Living with
Separation & Divorce

"*In more than 30 years as a family mediator, I have never come across a book that so clearly and helpfully addresses the full experience of divorce, touching on all areas of a family's life as they navigate a complex, emotion-filled and challenging transition. Fiona McAuslan and Peter Nicholson have created a readable, sensible and useful guide to separation and divorce. Couples who read and use the information and self-guided lessons in this book will be able to make the significant decisions regarding their children, finances and futures with greater self-confidence, heightened clarity and personal dignity. I intend to share this book with each family with whom I have the privilege to work and with my professional colleagues.*"

Michael Lang, family mediator, professor of Conflict Resolution and editor-in-chief of *Mediation Quarterly*, Sarasota, Florida

"*This is a great book. It does what the authors set out to do: it helps the two people who started a relationship together to deal with the end of that relationship. This help is provided in a clear, compassionate and practical way.*

The authors respect the role of the lawyer – which is to work for justice and particularly to ensure that the weak are made equal to the strong. They do not give legal or financial advice. But every lawyer should respect what is so well taught in this book – that talking, listening and all the new ideas of conflict resolution will, in most situations, be a better way than the adversarial way.

They teach about talking, which should be clear and truthful, and about good listening – listening with complete attention and with the heart. I like the way the authors have allowed some people's stories to be told. We all should listen but particularly to the voices of the children. Then we will understand what this book is about and why it is so very welcome."

Turlough O'Donnell, Senior Council

"This illustrated book is an essential and rich resource for all couples who are separating, in particular those who have children, as it helps them to understand and focus on what they each need to do to achieve a positive future, for themselves and for their children.

Separation and divorce can be a stressful, traumatic and/or conflict-ridden time and separating couples often need practical and timely assistance to negotiate the hurdles they face and to ensure that lasting plans are made that serve each of their best interests and the long-term interests and needs of their children.

The authors provide useful information about processes of change, decision making and negotiation, and various pathways that separating couples can take, and also provide comprehensive financial information, including information about budgets, assets, debts, pensions, wills and succession rights. They offer a range of choices for separating couples to consider in relation to the family home, their children and parenting arrangements, and illustrate their points with real-life stories of people who have experienced separation. The information and downloads they provide are also a very useful resource for service providers in this field of practice."

Dr Dale Bagshaw, visiting professor, School of Law and Business, National University of Ireland, Maynooth and adjunct associate professor, School of Psychology, Social Work and Social Policy, University of South Australia

"As a family mediator I have been involved in mediating family disputes around separation in Ireland for over a decade, and I wish this book had been available to my clients before now.

This book will be a friend and a guide to you; it will help you figure out how to take one step at a time. More importantly, you will feel the authors' support for you on these pages as you assess your choices. There may be times when you feel overwhelmed, or blinded by grief, anger, sadness, or fear of the future.

I will be recommending this book to all my future clients, and to their family members – who regularly contact me and seek advice about the best way to support their relative."

Julie McAuliffe, family mediator and conflict resolution consultant

"This is a well-thought-out and practical presentation. The reality of relationships ending is explored in a systemic way that includes great sensitivity to the parenting relationship."

Raymond O'Sullivan, clinical manager, Clanwilliam Institute

"This is an excellent guide: comprehensive and very accessible. It will be invaluable for couples going through the minefield of separation and divorce. It will help them focus on their children's needs and move forward with dignity and self-respect."

Polly Phillimore, national coordinator of the Family Mediation Services, Ireland

"The experience of separation or divorce is like dropping a stone into a still pond – the ripples keep going and reach much further than the centre. How people handle their separation has life-long effects, not just on them but on those around them, their children and their future relationships. This is a commonsense, practical guide which at the same time is full of compassion and understanding for everyone affected. It works throughout to help parents keep their children in mind and to protect their interests. It helps those at the centre of the turmoil develop perspective so that they can best plan for a future that they did not anticipate."

Freda McKittrick, head of Guardian ad Litem Service, Barnardos.

"This book steers away from hyperbole and is an essential handbook for all experiencing family problems."

Joe Maguire, family lawyer, collaborative practitioner and mediator

"Written in a style that is easily accessible, Fiona and Peter set out in this book the various paths that separating couples need to consider. The questions and exercises proposed at different stages in the reading will focus the mind of anyone going through a separation or divorce and increase their clarity about decision making during this difficult time. It is clear that the lessons to be learned from reading the book are drawn from Fiona's extensive experience in working with couples who are separating. This book will prove a lifesaver for many separating couples."

Delma Sweeney, programme director, Mediation and Conflict Intervention, School of Business, National University of Ireland, Maynooth

"This book deals authoritatively with both the emotional and the practical difficulties associated with separation and divorce, while at the same time reminding those going through the experience that it is possible to get through this dark period and come out stronger. It's written with great clarity and empathy and the illustrations complement this style. The role of mediation in helping separating couples work through their situation is explained and given its place alongside the other options, but there is no sense that people are being pushed in any particular direction."

Brendan Donaghy, editor of *Mediation Digest*

**Dedicated to Karen and Michael.
Thank you for all your support,
not just with the book but with everything.**

This book is also dedicated to the mediators, family lawyers and other professionals who work as peacemakers in the lives of separating families.

We would also like to thank Kelly Sheridan, our fantastic illustrator, Outsource Graphix, Blackhall Publishing, Polly Phillimore and The Family Mediation Service, The Family Support Agency, Delma Sweeney, Joe Maguire, George Hannan, The Clanwilliam Institute, Mairin Ni Fhaolain, Raymond O'Sullivan, Freda McKittrick, Turlough O'Donnell, Michael Lang, Elizabeth Brennan, Brendan Donaghy, Dr Dale Bagshaw, Eileen O'Connor, The Mediators' Institute of Ireland and Sandra Murphy. A special acknowledgment goes to Julie McAuliffe, whose compassion as a mediator has influenced this book hugely.

Living with
Separation
& Divorce

KITE BOOKS

Published by Kite Books
an imprint of Blackhall Publishing
Lonsdale House
Avoca Avenue
Blackrock
Co. Dublin
Ireland

info@blackhallpublishing.com
www.blackhallpublishing.com

ISBN: 978-1-84218-217-8

A catalogue record for this book is available from the British Library.

Desktop publishing by Outsource Graphix Ltd.
info@ogx.ie
www.ogx.ie

Printed in Northern Ireland by GPS Colour Graphics Ltd.

CONTENTS

VISIT US ONLINE...

Visit us online for useful downloads, including:
- Budget sheets
- Parenting plan
- Outline of separation agreement

You can also see the views of and interviews with other professionals in the fields of mediation, law, finance and children, as well as other useful information and tips.

www.livingwithseparation.com

INTRODUCTION

Living with Separation & Divorce is a guide to help both you and your partner through the journey of separation.

It is a simple manual to help and direct your mutual problem solving.

It will NOT tell you what to do.
It will NOT make judgments about how you have lived your life.
It will NOT give you legal or financial advice.

When an individual or couple have decided that they cannot continue in a relationship, the inevitability of separation brings with it a number of choices that both people will have to live with for the rest of their lives. These choices also affect the people around them, especially their children, if they have children.

Although instances of separation and divorce have dramatically increased over the last number of years, most people in this situation only experience separation in the context of a serious long-term relationship once. There is no road map to a successful separation as there are so many different elements to consider and no real winners, just people trying to get on with their lives.

We wrote this book to show couples that they can choose how to manage their separation.

In her work with couples, Fiona is constantly impressed by the courage of the men and women she meets, who find the determination not to fight every step of the way or, indeed, to stop the fight that they had been embroiled in for years. They find a way to put aside the hurt and the anger in order to create a new start for themselves and their family.

These people are the inspiration for those of you starting out on this difficult path, not those of us who claim to be "experts in the field".

They show us all that it is possible to change the way we talk to each other and negotiate. We do not need to win at the expense of the other person. We can see the bigger picture and focus on a solution that gives a future for everyone.

Will everyone get what they want? No, of course not; it is not possible, as a couple who once shared their lives are now dividing up everything from custody of children to the home, finance and even pensions.

No matter what process you choose for negotiating your separation or divorce, you will not be perfectly happy with the outcome. How you treat each other during the process will have a bigger impact on your life than you may realise.

It may be impossible to imagine relations between yourself and your partner ever being civil, but the future lies in your hands. Read this book, take one day at a time and remember that, despite everything, the best future is the one in which everyone in the family can live a good life.

ABOUT THE AUTHORS

Fiona A. McAuslan holds a Master's in Mediation and Conflict Resolution Studies from University College Dublin. She is an experienced mediator and conflict coach with many years' experience working with family, workplace and school conflicts. She works in the Irish Family Mediation Service and Clanwilliam Institute and is an accredited practitioner mediator with the Mediators' Institute of Ireland. Fiona has published *The S.A.L.T. Programme: A Conflict Resolution Education Programme for Primary Schools*. She lives in North County Dublin with her husband Michael, and her children Sarah and Ben.

Peter Nicholson is a communications specialist and has built a very successful marketing and visual communications business over the last fifteen years. Peter and Fiona met whilst working on the S.A.L.T. programme and they have continued to work together on many other projects. He is married to Karen, and they have two children, Patrick and Ailish.

Over the last number of years, Fiona and Peter have published a number of self-help books for children in the *Resolving Books* series. These books cover many subjects such as bullying, anger, sibling rivalry, bereavement and separation. For more information on the *Resolving Books,* visit www.resolvingbooks.com.

The illustrations in this book are by Kelly Sheridan, who has worked with Fiona and Peter on a number of other projects in the past.

As you start reading this book, you may be
feeling overwhelmed by all you face
and all the advice you are getting.

At the end of the day, two people who started a relationship together now have to deal with the end of that relationship.

This book will help you focus on what you each need to do to achieve a positive future after your separation.

FLOWCHART MAP

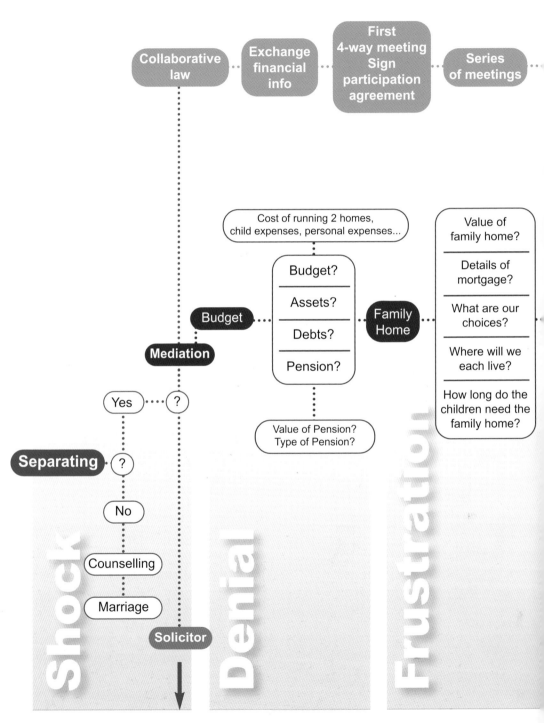

Collaborative law

Exchange financial info

First 4-way meeting Sign participation agreement

Series of meetings

Cost of running 2 homes, child expenses, personal expenses...

Value of family home?

Budget?

Assets?

Debts?

Pension?

Details of mortgage?

What are our choices?

Where will we each live?

How long do the children need the family home?

Budget

Family Home

Mediation

Yes

?

Value of Pension? Type of Pension?

Separating

?

No

Counselling

Marriage

Solicitor

Shock

Denial

Frustration

COLLABORATIVE LAW PATH

Separation agreement

Final Agreement

Judicial separation agreement

Consent to divorce

MEDIATION PATH

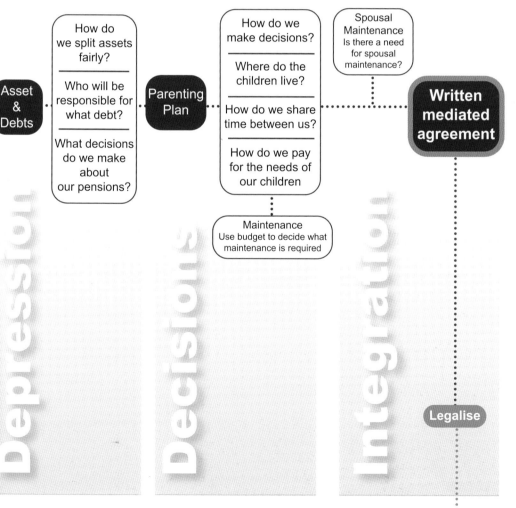

How do we split assets fairly?

Who will be responsible for what debt?

What decisions do we make about our pensions?

Asset & Debts

Parenting Plan

How do we make decisions?

Where do the children live?

How do we share time between us?

How do we pay for the needs of our children

Spousal Maintenance
Is there a need for spousal maintenance?

Written mediated agreement

Maintenance
Use budget to decide what maintenance is required

Depression

Decisions

Integration

Legalise

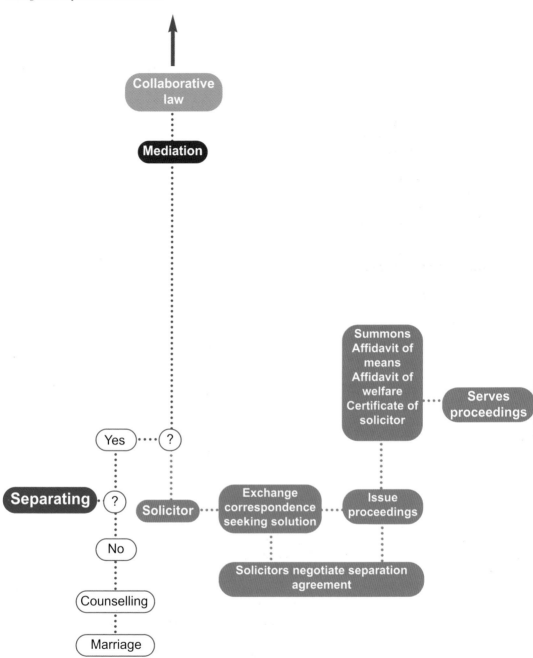

LEGAL PATH

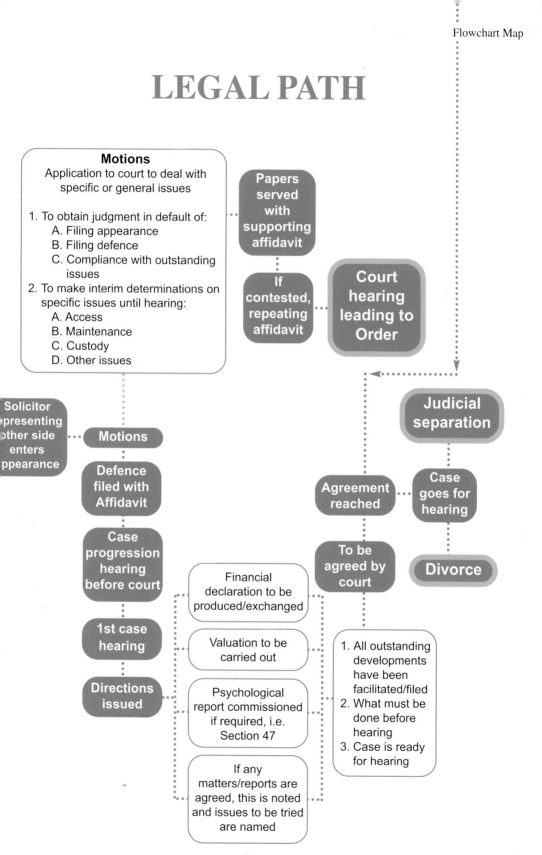

Motions
Application to court to deal with specific or general issues

1. To obtain judgment in default of:
   A. Filing appearance
   B. Filing defence
   C. Compliance with outstanding issues
2. To make interim determinations on specific issues until hearing:
   A. Access
   B. Maintenance
   C. Custody
   D. Other issues

Papers served with supporting affidavit

If contested, repeating affidavit

Court hearing leading to Order

Solicitor representing other side enters appearance

Motions

Defence filed with Affidavit

Case progression hearing before court

1st case hearing

Directions issued

Judicial separation

Agreement reached

Case goes for hearing

To be agreed by court

Divorce

Financial declaration to be produced/exchanged

Valuation to be carried out

Psychological report commissioned if required, i.e. Section 47

If any matters/reports are agreed, this is noted and issues to be tried are named

1. All outstanding developments have been facilitated/filed
2. What must be done before hearing
3. Case is ready for hearing

SEPARATING

The break down of a relationship is a hard and heartrending experience. The person you are now parting from was once the person you thought you would spend the rest of your life with. As the relationship disintegrates, it can mean the end of the dreams and expectations you both had for the future.

We do not expect things to end up like this.

It does not really matter whether you both have agreed to part by mutual consent or if one of you has decided without the consent of the other. There is pain on all sides.

Yet, you still have lives to lead and futures to rebuild. If you have children, there is the ongoing parenting to plan for. How do you work this out together? How can it be possible to talk to this other person, who you used to know so well?

While it is not easy, it is possible to find a way forward. There are many divorced couples and families who live positive lives beyond the experience of separation. It may take time, but it is possible to regain a good and happy life.

Ask yourself about where you want to be in five years. What will you want to say about how you and your family coped with the separation?

Try this...

Imagine yourself in five years' time talking to a friend:

"We separated five years ago and we..."

Finishing this sentence will help you to think about HOW you want the separation to proceed between you and your partner.

THE PERSONAL EXPERIENCE OF SEPARATING

It is widely recognised that separation is one of the most stressful personal experiences anyone can ever go through. The feelings you are having, as part of this experience, are real and normal. As human beings we feel vulnerable, fearful, confused and angry when crisis events like this happen to us. Many health professionals have worked over the years to understand how we respond to such crises and what we can do to help ourselves come through them.

Elizabeth Kúbler-Ross developed a number of stages that most of us go through when we are faced with change (see the following page).

While this is a general description of the stages most people experience, it will not quite fit everyone. However, it can be helpful to know that how you are feeling at this time is part of a transition you are going through. Things will change and things will get better.

As you can see, there are some stages that make good decision making very hard to do. Where do you think you are at the moment? Are you too angry with your partner to negotiate a balanced and fair separation agreement? Can you summon up the energy to think through all of the issues you have to face?

If these are real questions for you, it may be a good idea to talk to someone you trust about supporting you at this time and to defer the really big decisions until you are able to think in a more balanced way about your future.

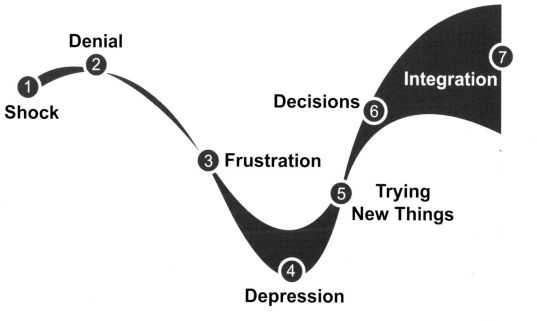

Stage 1: **Shock** and surprise in response to the event or change. "I can't believe what's happened!"

Stage 2: **Denial** of change and finding ways to prove that it isn't happening. Sticking your head in the sand and reassuring yourself that it isn't really happening.

Stage 3: On the way down, and experiencing anger, **frustration** and apathy. Often a tendency to blame everyone and lash out at them. Still no acceptance of the change.

Stage 4: Hitting rock bottom and experiencing **depression** and apathy. Everything seems pointless.

Stage 5: Stage 4 is so depressing that most of us start to pull ourselves out of it. This is where you will start to **try out new things**.

Stage 6: **Deciding** what works and what doesn't work. Accepting change and beginning to feel more optimistic and enthusiastic.

Stage 7: At this stage, you will **integrate** the change into your life so it becomes part of your norm – the new you.

SEPARATING: A TIME OF CHANGE

The type of change that separation and divorce brings is usually quite unwelcome. Even for those who know it is the right decision, it is a time of turmoil. The trail of anger, bitterness and expensive litigation is very far away from the optimism and joy of the marriage ceremony.

How we deal with the change is very much affected by how we have handled crises in the past. There is a sense of increased vulnerability but we can draw on our past to help us at this time.

Try this...

1. Can you think of a time in your past when you were in crisis?
2. What did you do that you would not want to repeat?
3. What did you do that helped you?
4. What ultimately helped you to get through this time?
5. What did you learn from this time that could help you now?

We cannot stop change happening, but we do have a choice about how we cope with it. Change can be a time for opportunity and growth. We can learn something new that helps us cope and, ultimately, we have this new maturity to help us in the future.

In five years' time you will look back at this time as a challenging episode in your life. It will have passed, however painfully, but it will have passed.

HOW WE MAKE DECISIONS

Quite often we hear people talking about making "rational decisions" or leaving "feelings to one side". This is not possible, as our brains are wired to take feelings into account.

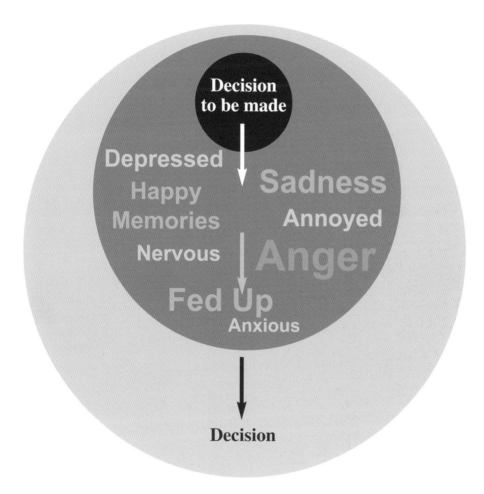

WE FEEL BEFORE WE THINK...

Nobody thinks without their feelings being involved. As a human being, no matter how clinical you believe your decision making is, you are still influenced by your emotions, experiences and values.

When the thinking part of our brain starts to think about making a decision, our emotional centre has already acted and affected how we think.

This has a big effect on us when we are dealing with someone we have such a strong emotional history with.

Try this...

1. Draw a picture of your family home (it does not need to be a masterpiece!).
2. Write down on the page all the feelings you have about this place.
3. Write beside the picture the decisions you may need to make about it.
4. As you are doing this, can you sense your feelings as you write down each possible decision? Each decision impacts us in a different but very real way.
5. Which feelings are helpful and which are clouding your vision?

When we are making decisions in such a difficult emotional environment, we need to take time to reflect on how our feelings are affecting the decisions we make.

ANXIETY IN DECISION MAKING

When we are coping with difficult situations, we can come into our own and "perform well". We find it challenging but we can rise to the occasion. However, when things get too much for us, we reach a tipping point. At this point, the activity in our brain moves to the emotional centre, and our thinking and language centres flood with adrenaline and switch off.

The effect on us is that we freeze. We cannot think straight. All goes blank and we start to sweat. At the very point we need to be at our best, we feel panicked and unable to cope.

This is a real physiological reaction that, when it happens, can floor us. How many times have you looked back on a meeting and thought, "if only had kept my cool" or "If only I had said that." It happens to us all.

So what can we do? All performers prepare before difficult sports events or concerts. This helps them to stay cool in the heat of the moment. When you know you have a difficult meeting to face, be as well prepared as you can. Take time to reflect on what to expect.

Before the meeting, ask yourself these questions:

1. What do I expect of myself in this meeting?

2. What do I expect of the other party?

3. What are my aims?

4. What do I need to do to fulfill these aims?

5. What do I think the aims of the other person will be?

6. What and how do I need to prepare?

If you know you have something important to say in the meeting, write it down and practise several times in the mirror beforehand. Try out different ways of saying it and think of what responses you may receive. Now practise how you would respond. It is very rare that all will go exactly as you envision, but rehearsing like this will give you confidence and fine-tune your skills. You will be ready for anything and your brain will be less likely to reach its tipping point.

In the meeting:
If you feel yourself panicking, take three deep breaths and focus on staying calm before you respond.

After the meeting, ask yourself:

1. What did I do well?

2. What could I have done better?

3. How can I do things better next time?

4. Do I feel alright?

5. If not, what would help me at the moment?

After this, take time to relax. Do something that you enjoy. Let yourself recuperate before returning to your daily routine.

Try this...

1. Keep a notebook with you and write down your thoughts, the issues that are important to you and your feelings as to how each meeting has gone.
2. Use the above questions to help you organise your thoughts.
3. Build up a record that you can use to map your progress.
4. Look back at your notes before you go to your next meeting.

WHY DO I HAVE TO BE THE REASONABLE ONE?

So, you are reading this and thinking, "It is all very well me doing all of this but I am not the unreasonable one here!" Maybe that is true; however, we can only manage ourselves. We cannot force someone else to change. In fact, quite often, the more we try, the less success we have.

It can be the ultimate frustration to feel as if we are constantly on the receiving end of someone's unreasonable behaviour. Nothing we can do seems to make the situation easier and we feel as if we are permanently giving way in order to keep the peace. If this is your situation, it is more important than ever to stay calm and not to lose your cool. Be realistic about your own expectations and, if you need to stand up to the other person's behaviour, seek support to help you.

There is a saying, "the ultimate revenge is living a good life of your own." Maybe this is a good focus.

SEPARATION: A JOINT EXPERIENCE

You may feel as if you have nothing in common with your separating partner, but the truth is you each rely on the other to negotiate a fair and equitable agreement for your separation. The more you row about each issue, the more unsolvable it becomes.

Ruminating over the hurt helps anger to build up and, as anger builds, thoughts become more intense. Views become more convincing and you become more sure that you are right. Forgiveness is out of the question and revenge becomes all-consuming. This state of invincibility and power creates a feeling of security.

The only problem is... the same thing is happening to your partner. This stream of angry thoughts that feeds the cycle we are describing is also present in them. This ability to justify yourself is also in your partner. This sense of righteous indignation is also present in your partner.

If you decide to fight every step of the way, then you have to accept the consequence of how the other person reacts to you. Maybe there is good reason for you to be annoyed, but, when it comes to negotiating your separation, while you cannot force your partner to change, you need to think about how your behaviour is affecting the outcome of your separation.

The truth is, if you want things to be fair, then you have to be fair yourself. The reality is that the person you are fighting with and separating from is the person that is most influential in how your separation will work out. You are in this together.

The level of crisis you feel is all part of separating. You still have a choice in how you behave.

Try this...

1. Think about the assumptions you have about your partner.
2. What has brought you to this conclusion?
3. Do these assumptions affect how you feel about your partner?
4. Think about the assumptions that your partner may have about you.
5. How do you think they have reached those conclusions?
6. How are these assumptions affecting matters between you?
7. What does this mean for any future agreement?
8. How could you think of things differently and how would that help?

Don't lose sight of the fact that you still have some control over your life and you have a future to build.

CAN WE TALK?

Such a question can often be met with wry laughter. "If we were able to talk we would not be in this situation!" This, of course, is true, yet there are important issues to be dealt with and they will have to be sorted one way or another.

It is easy to think that handing all the difficult conversations and decisions over to someone else is the best thing to do; that it would cut out all the difficulty of the arguments, the hurtful comments or long silences. However, take time to think if this is the right course for you. Do you want a third party to make decisions for you?

If you are parents, what type of relationship do you want to have for your children? Is it possible for you and your partner to talk about any issues? Do you agree on any matters?

If you can discuss and agree them between you, it is ultimately these conversations that will affect the months and maybe years following your decision to separate.

Try this...

Think about what you and your ex-partner need to agree on. How would you discuss these issues if you were in a business partnership?

1. Arrange and agree a time and place (neutral venue) to meet.
2. Decide beforehand:
    - What you are going to discuss, i.e. maintenance, parenting plan.
    - How long the meeting will be.
3. Don't try and cover too much. A small success can make a big difference.
4. Make an agreement to treat each other with respect and to avoid provoking each other.

Remember that neither of you will get everything you want. It can be useful to use a 70% rule. If both of you are 70% happy, you have reached a workable agreement.

WHO TO TALK WITH

This idea of talking can seem like a big task, but, if there are issues to sort out, there are a number of basic choices as to how to do this:

KITCHEN TABLE
You sit down together and work out a plan between you.

MEDIATION
You find someone to help you sit down together and work out a plan.

SOLICITOR
You each ask someone else to meet and sort it out on your behalf.

JUDGE
You ask someone else to decide for you.

The earlier you can come to an agreement in the process, the better.

HOW TO TALK TO EACH OTHER

At what point in this process can both of you come to an agreement on all the issues around your separation? It might help you to think about how you made decisions in the past.

1. When things were good between you, how did you and your partner make decisions?
    Did you sit down and make them together or did you each have areas of responsibility?

2. When you had a disagreement, what happened?
    How did you patch things up?

3. Can you think of a time when the two of you made a difficult but good decision?
    How did you do it?
    What did each of you contribute to the process?
    What did each of you do well?

4. Would it be possible to use any of your past experience of making decisions together now?

NEGOTIATION SKILLS

We all use our negotiation skills every day, from deciding where to go out with friends to working with colleagues through to parenting our children. Our ability to negotiate relies on:

1. Our ability to articulate our own needs and interests while developing an understanding for those of the other party. This is called empathy.

When we empathise, even in conflict, we are creating the understanding we need to build the foundation for lasting agreement or resolution.

2. Our ability to effectively communicate with the other parties.

Communication is a two-way process that involves speaking clearly on our own behalf and listening to the other parties. This means we have to find a way of talking about our own feelings, needs and interests, and also a way of listening to the other person to understand their feelings, needs and interests as well.

3. Our ability to problem solve.

Good problem solving is the key to a long-lasting agreement. If you find a way of understanding the problem and working on a good solution, rather than staying in the constant cycle of rowing and stalemate, then you start to feel as if you are moving forward. The process used involves information gathering, brainstorming ideas based on the information gathered, prioritising the options, reality-checking the choices and making an informed decision.

4. Our ability to sustain the agreement.

Any agreement is only as good as its viability. There is no point in agreeing to something that is in reality not going to work. This exacerbates rather than resolves conflict. Possibly the most successful part of collaborative negotiation is its success at producing longer-lasting agreements. If you have forced an agreement on someone else, how likely are they to wholeheartedly want it to work?

NEGOTIATING IN CONFLICT

Conflict can involve a lot of difficult emotions that can make negotiating difficult. The feelings we have towards each other can be so overwhelming that the idea of negotiating together seems impossible.

There are two basic psychological shifts that we need to make to move from combat to collaboration.

1. We need to feel we can voice what matters to us and be heard. Sometimes this is simply based on feeling that the other person is listening to us with respect, but more often it is a combination of this and our ability to articulate our needs and interests honestly and clearly.

2. We need to be able to acknowledge that the other party has needs, interests and an emotional landscape, which matter as much as our own.

DECIDING IF NEGOTIATION IS SUITED TO THE SITUATION

Ask yourself the following questions:

1. What will happen if I walk away right now?
2. Will this difficulty go away on its own?
3. Can I deal with this person right now? If not, what needs to happen for me to be able to do so?
4. If I stay and listen to what they have to say, will I learn something?
5. If I stay and tell them what I think and feel, will they learn something?
6. If we manage to sort this out, what will my life be like?
7. What could I gain from trying to sort this out now?
8. What could I lose from sorting this out now?
9. What could I gain by choosing another way of sorting it out?
10. What could I lose by choosing another way of sorting it out?

When we ask these questions, we help ourselves to see the bigger picture. By looking at our needs in this way, we begin to focus on how to truly resolve the issues that concern us and our family. Whether we decide to negotiate or not, we benefit from knowing we have given it careful consideration.

NEGOTIATION TOOLKIT

Understanding your negotiating relationship

It can be helpful to reflect on the nature of the negotiating relationship you and your separating partner share and how you can understand it better for future meetings. This time of reflection can act as a preparation which will help you cope better with the meetings and enhance the productive nature of the negotiations.

Use these questions to help you prepare:

- What could your partner say that would upset you?
- How would this affect you?
- What feelings would you have?
- How are you likely to interpret their motive?
- What would the consequences be if you reacted to them?

Now answer these questions:

- What could you say that might upset your ex-partner?
- How do you think this would affect them?
- What feelings do you think they would have?
- How are they likely to interpret your motive?
- What would the consequences be if they reacted to you?

Now think of these questions:

- What are the issues that you want to resolve?
- What are the issues that your separating partner may want to resolve?

- What resolution do you really want for these issues?
- What resolution do you really want for your relationship?

- What do you think your partner's ideal resolution is?
- What do you think your partner really wants for your relationship?

- What options are there to help you resolve these issues and reach agreement?

The options:

Using this table, grade possible options according to your preference:

Write in the Issue:	*Family home*	*Weekly schedule*	*Maintenance*	etc...
My preferred option:				
This is acceptable:				
I could live with:				
I would rather not:				

Using this table, grade the options you think your separating partner would choose:

Write in the Issue:	*Family home*	*Weekly schedule*	*Maintenance*	etc...
Their preferred option:				
This is acceptable:				
They could live with:				
They would rather not:				

What are you both likely to agree on?

- If you have children, what would your children appreciate most about any agreement you make?
- What can you do or say to help your family move towards a fair agreement?
- What do you hope your separating partner can do or say to help your family move towards a fair agreement?
- What would you be prepared to give up to reach a fair agreement?
- What do you think your partner might give up to reach a fair agreement?

So, what are the main things that have to be sorted out at this time?

They are the same matters you have been dealing with over your life:
- Where to live.
- How to manage money.
- How to raise the children.
- How to pay for their education, health and upkeep.
- How to provide for old age.
- Making good decisions about assets and debts.

Now you are changing the way you and your partner manage these matters.

Remember that you are the expert on your own life. You know more than anyone else about what makes you happy and how you want to live your life.

No matter who helps you, be they a mediator, a solicitor or a judge, it will be you and your ex-partner who finally make the decision to agree and move on.

Here are some of the people who help couples with their separation agreement:

Mediators:
- Help couples negotiate their own agreement.
- Will not make judgments.
- Are not experts who will give advice.
- Are conflict resolution professionals who will help couples stop the fight.
- Will write up a mediated agreement.

Solicitors:
- Give legal advice.
- Will give their opinion about what may happen in court.
- Carry out certain legal functions (legalise separation, transfer deeds of family home, look after wills, etc.).
- Guide you through the legal process.

Judge:
- Listens to both sides and makes a final decision based on both you and your partner's arguments and the facts put before him or her.

Remember: a judge does not take sides and may not agree with your solicitor.

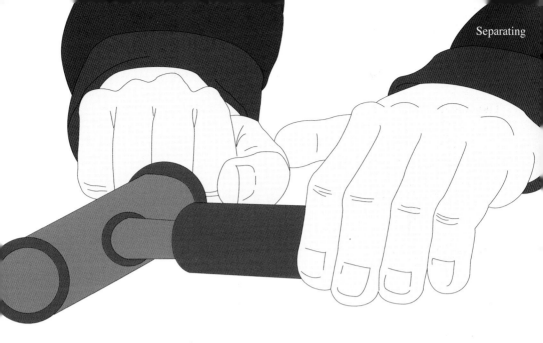

LEGAL SEPARATION

When you get married you make a legal contract called a marriage contract. This means you have formed a legal union with your spouse and, if this is to be broken, it has to be done so legally.

The legal dissolution of marriage is called divorce. This has to be granted by a court and is called a Decree of Divorce. The accepted reasons for such a decree change from country to country, but, wherever you are in the world, there are a number of issues common to most jurisdictions that need to be dealt with at this time. These are the issues covered in this book. While they can be agreed between you informally, you will need to legalise these agreements if you wish to divorce.

Divorce proceedings come under family law and this means there are some differences in how the court makes its decisions:

1. The court will make a decision on how the assets are distributed in the context of the separation or divorce. It is not simply bound to decide who owns what.
2. The court will make decisions based on the future needs and responsibilities of the family members.
3. The court will endeavour to put the care and welfare of the children first when making such decisions.

Who do I go to for legal advice?

The person you need to go to is a family law solicitor. They are experts in family law and understand how to advise and represent you.

What will happen?

In the first interview, the solicitor will ask you some questions to establish the basic facts of your situation. Be as clear and honest as you can. Family law solicitors are experienced in helping families at times like this.

What do I need to bring?

- Proof of your date and place of marriage.
- Names and dates of birth of your children.
- Information of any agreement you have already made with your spouse.
- If you have a mediated agreement then bring a copy of this.

How much will it cost?

Prices vary and it will depend on what the solicitor needs to do on your behalf. When you make the initial appointment, ask about the charges. Solicitors are obliged to give you a written note of their fees. If they cannot be precise, they are obliged to give you an estimate of costs and an outline of how their fees are structured.

What does a solicitor do?

After establishing the facts based on your instructions, your solicitor will advise you on your legal rights as he or she sees them. He or she will then represent you.

WHICH PROCESS WILL WORK BEST FOR YOU?

The main processes for negotiating a separation and divorce are mediation, collaborative practice and the traditional court route. Although they deal with separation in different ways, sometimes couples will use more than one of these routes, if their circumstances require it. Couples can use a combination of these routes.

To make the most of any of these processes, take time to learn about what they have to offer and to find a professional in the field who is right for your circumstances.

MEDIATION

What is mediation for separating couples?

Mediation is a service that helps married and non-married couples who have decided to separate or divorce to negotiate their own terms of agreement, taking into account the needs and interests of all involved. It allows people to make their own decisions. It is possible between mediation sessions to take legal, financial or other advice from professionals. This can help you make informed decisions within the process.

How can mediation help?

Mediation encourages the separating couple to co-operate with each other. This means that any agreement made is mutually acceptable to both and more likely to be honoured by both. Any issue can be negotiated.

What is the mediator's role?

The mediator will see the couple together and look at the issues to be discussed and agreed on. They will help to create a climate in which neither party dominates. Both parties will be encouraged to participate fully and in good faith.

The mediator will create and maintain an atmosphere of co-operation and will help couples to deal with difficult emotional issues that can prevent them reaching agreement.

How does the process work?

In the first session, the mediator explains the process and will talk you through what to expect. Both parties attend together, although sometimes the mediator may want to see you separately. Discussions are confidential and the mediator does not take sides.

What will be the end result?

Most mediations end with a written document that sets out all the details of what has been agreed.

This can then be taken to solicitors to be drawn up into a legal document.

Mediation promotes good communication and co-operation and reduces bitterness and distress. Parents are helped to remain as "parenting partners" and are encouraged to negotiate parenting plans that suit their particular circumstances. Parents are helped to manage conflict in a way that protects the best interests of their children.

COLLABORATIVE PRACTICE

How does it work?

The couple takes part in a series of meetings with their two collaborative lawyers. Usually, there are between four and eight meetings. At the start, a participation agreement is signed by all participants including the lawyers. This is a contract which agrees to share information freely and frankly. It also provides that, if the process fails, the lawyers will not participate in any contested proceedings involving the couple before the courts. This is important for the final outcome of the meetings.

If either or both of you need the advice of another professional, such as an accountant, child specialist or family therapist, they will be involved in the process as well.

What is the difference between collaborative practice and mediation?

In mediation, the mediator cannot give either party legal advice. They support both of you to make your own decisions. In collaborative practice, it is the job of the lawyers to work with their own clients, giving them legal advice as required, and, where agreement is reached, to take all the steps necessary to implement the agreement, by applying to court for a Consent Order, if necessary.

What kind of information and documents do I need to provide?

You will be asked to provide similar documents and financial information as for the mediation or the more formal court process (see Chapter 2: Finance). However, this will be in a formal and vouched format, which can be used after the process, if the process is not successful.

What happens if you think your partner does not provide the right information?

In collaborative practice, the solicitor has to withdraw if his or her client is being less than fully honest, or is participating in the process with less than full good faith.

Negotiating an agreement

All parties work to reach an agreement, which they believe will be durable. If an agreement is reached, the couple can request the court to grant Orders for Judicial Separation or Divorce.

Collaborative law is a process, available in many countries, in which both of you have specially trained lawyers who help you negotiate your separation agreement out of court. All agree to work together respectfully, honestly and in good faith to try to find solutions that help both parties. Lawyers who take part in the collaborative law process cannot represent you in contested proceedings against your spouse.

TRADITIONAL COURT ROUTE

How does it work?

Decisions in court are made by a judge, after listening to the arguments put to him or her by each side. The judge's decision is known as a Rule of Court and is binding for both parties. In some cases it is possible to appeal the decision. This will depend on the circumstances and you will need to take good legal advice before deciding to do this.

Most family law proceedings seeking separation or divorce take place in the Circuit Court.

What is different about choosing this route?

The main difference is that you do not talk to your partner in any of the meetings. Your solicitor and then, when you go to court, your barrister will do the talking for you. It is a longer and more expensive process and also tends to be more adversarial. This means that, because each side is arguing their case in front of the judge, it is hard to keep any issue between you from getting caught up in the argument.

Does the whole separation agreement have to go through court?

No, it can vary. It is quite often the case that a judge will refer some cases to mediation, where they see this as relevant. In particular, mediation is seen as being an option for decisions on parenting, even when other matters remain before the court.

When should I go to court?

This will be up to you with the advice of your solicitor. There can be special reasons for going to court. For example, if you need a Safety or Barring Order or there is a threat of assets being depleted or children being deported from the State. However, it can be a difficult decision to make. It is possible to represent yourself in court, although this is not usually advised. Having the right kind of legal advice to navigate the legal system can save a lot of time and worry.

How do I find out more?

Each country has a different legal system. The first thing you need to do is consult a family law solicitor, who will advise you on what to do next. Remember to ask for a break down of the fees, including the cost of a barrister, and a description of what to expect.

What kind of information do I need to provide?

You will be asked to provide similar information as for the mediation and collaborative law processes. It will be important for you to verify what you say with the right documentation.

The family law courts are there to help families who are in dispute and need a court to decide their future. They are designed to be less intimidating than the High Court and try to make family friendly decisions. Barristers put their arguments before the judge and then he or she makes a decision. The decision will be based on the laws governing the issues under dispute and influenced by case law already established.

LEGAL TERMS

A **Decree of Divorce** allows both spouses to remarry. A court can grant a divorce in Ireland, under the following conditions:

- The parties must have been living apart from one another for a period amounting to four out of the previous five years before the application is made.
- There must be no reasonable prospect of reconciliation.
- The court is satisfied that proper arrangements must have been made or will be made for the spouse and any dependent members of the family, such as children of either party and other relatives.

Parenting Terminology

Guardianship is the legal responsibility that parents have to make decisions and look after their children. Married parents are automatically joint guardians of their children. Neither separation nor divorce changes this. In some countries non-married fathers need to apply for guardianship.

Custody refers to the day-to-day care, residency and upbringing of children who are regarded as dependent children (children who are under the age of eighteen). One parent can be granted custody. If this happens, the children live permanently with the parent who has custody and the other parent is granted access to the children at agreed times, which can include overnight. It is possible for parents to have joint custody of their children after separation or divorce. In this case, the children would spend an equal amount of time with each parent. Parents can agree on and arrange this.

Access refers to the right of the parent with whom the child does not reside to spend time with the child. It can include overnight stays, either occasionally, on alternate weekends or during school holidays, and allows the parent and child to go on holidays together. The parents may agree informally between themselves the arrangements for custody and access to the child.

If agreement cannot be reached, either parent may make an application to the court. The court will then decide which parent will have custody of the child and what access the non-custodial parent will have.

The child is considered to be the most important person for the court in how it makes its decision. It is seen as a child's right to spend time with both parents and access will only be denied if the court believes that it is not in the best interests of the child. The court can set out the schedule for visits and can order supervised access, if it thinks it is necessary. This type of access is where another adult is present during visits.

Maintenance Terminology

Maintenance is the name given to the legal payment both or either spouse has to pay to maintain each other and any children they have. Maintenance can be paid weekly or monthly, or in a lump sum.

Voluntary maintenance is an informal agreement to pay maintenance. It can work well but can be hard to work out. Informal agreements can include a transfer of property or a lump-sum payment. This does not stop the possibility of applying for a Maintenance Order through the courts at some time in the future.

Maintenance Orders are orders made by the court; if the separating couple cannot agree on maintenance, either party can apply to court for a Maintenance Order. In general, maintenance can be awarded to a spouse for their own benefit or for the benefit of a child who is under the age of 18, or 23 if the child is in full-time education. If you believe you have special circumstances then it is important to check with a solicitor.

Enforcing a Maintenance Order: If a spouse fails to comply with a court order and does not pay the amount awarded by the court, the court can enforce the order. For example, the court can arrange for the money to be deducted from the spouse's income.

Maintenance following separation and divorce: In some countries, a spouse can apply to the court for a Maintenance Order or a variation on a Maintenance Order after the divorce has been granted. The court will consider this application.

Family Home Terminology

A **family home**, in legal terms, is the house that family members live in most of the time and consider their principal home. If a couple cannot agree on who will occupy or own the family home, the court can make an order. This order is called a **Property Adjustment Order**.

When the court makes this order, it will have considered all of the family circumstances, including the welfare of a dependent spouse and children. The court order will state:

> - Who has the right to live in the family home and for how long.
> - Who has ownership rights in the family home and what share each spouse owns.

If there are children, the spouse who the children live with will often be given the right to live in the family home until the youngest child reaches age 18 or 23. This is seen as providing a sense of security and continuity for the children.

A court can **order that the house be sold** and the equity divided between the two spouses in designated percentages. It can also order that the sale be deferred for a specified period of time, or it can transfer the house into joint names or into the sole name of one spouse. If the house is held under a tenancy, the court can order the transfer of that tenancy.

In some countries there are laws preventing the sale of the family home unless both spouses agree to it. This is sometimes known as the **Family Law Protection Act**.

Pensions and Property Terminology

A **pension** can be one of the most valuable assets for a separating couple to own. A court can have the power to order that the pension be divided whatever way it considers appropriate. This order is called a **Pension Adjustment Order**.

It is important for each spouse to know the full details of any pension before a divorce is finalised. Pensions can be very complicated and it is important to get advice from a specialist in pensions before any final decision is made.

Succession rights are the rights to inherit a person's property on their death. The share to which a spouse is entitled is often called "a legal right share". Once a Decree of Divorce is granted, the parties are no longer married to each other and succession rights are automatically finished. A divorced spouse can make an application to court seeking a share of their former spouse's estate. There are, however, time limits on how long after the divorce this can apply.

Other Special Order Terminology

A **Safety Order** is an order of the court which stops the violent person from carrying out further violence or threats of violence. It does not oblige the person to leave the family home. If the person lives separately already then it prevents them from watching or being near your home.

A **Barring Order** is an order which requires the violent person to leave the family home. The order also prohibits the person from carrying out further violence or threats of violence, and from watching or being near your home.

Child abduction is the term used to describe a situation where a child is removed from the person who has the legal right to custody of that child, without that person's consent.

DOMESTIC ABUSE

What is domestic abuse?

> *"Domestic abuse is a pattern of behaviour used by one person (most often a male) to control and dominate another (most often female) in an intimate relationship. Domestic abuse can also be inflicted on men by women or in same-sex relationships, but the most common occurrence is of women by men."*
>
> – Definition taken from Barnardos parenting leaflets

The most important aspect of separation is for you and your children to be as safe as possible throughout. Take time to think about what is the best way forward. It is not always easy to work out what to do.

Talk to a support person. There are many support groups and counsellors who are experienced in listening and supporting individuals at a time like this.

Before you decide on any final plan, it is worth contacting your local Citizens Information Centre/Citizen's Advice Centre to receive advice and support.

Take one day at a time. There can be many emotions running through your head, which can make it hard to think and plan.

Can you ask your partner to leave the home or is it safer for you to go?

If you decide to leave, is there someone who will provide a safe place for you? Maybe there is a local women's refuge you can contact? Alternatively, can you afford a B&B or hotel?

Do you have access to money? If not, there may be emergency payments available from your community welfare officer or the Department of Social Protection.

Can the law help me at this time?

A lot of countries have laws designed to help protect people from domestic abuse. If you decide you need to take legal action, consult with a solicitor who has experience in dealing with such cases. The legal action that will be right for you will depend on your own particular circumstances. Questions to ask include:

- What are the main laws that will protect me and my children?
- How will they do this?
- How can these laws apply to me?
- What are their limits?

- How long does it take for a court order to be granted?
- Can an order be renewed?
- Does a court order stop my partner from seeing the children?

- How much does it cost?
- Can I apply for free legal aid?
- Is support available to help me get ready for court?

What will happen with parenting in the future?

It can be difficult to negotiate informal arrangements where domestic abuse has been present and it may be necessary to go to court to seek more formal arrangements.

Will mediation help at this time?

Mediation may be suitable for your family but, equally, it may not. When you first contact the mediator it will be important to discuss your circumstances with them so that they can support you in the right way.

What can I do to make the parenting arrangements as safe as possible?

1. Ask someone else to be with you, such as a friend or family member, when you are in your ex-partner's company.

2. Arrange the exchange of the children in a public place.

3. Apply to the court to make any changes to the arrangements.

ALCOHOL AND DRUG ABUSE

There are many support agencies who work with people in a non-judgmental and caring way. This support can mean the difference between coping and not coping over the first weeks and months of a separation. A good place to start accessing that support is through your local doctor's surgery. They can help you find the right services for you and your family.

Some things to think about:

It is important to attend mediation, legal or court sessions with a clear head, being able to represent your views well and negotiate your future effectively.

If you have children and, as part of the parenting plan, you will be looking after them on your own, you will need to be able to care for them fully. If there is any doubt that you can do this, because of drink or drugs, you may run the risk of losing this time with your children.

If you are worried that your partner will be unable to take care of the children because of drinking or drug use, it is important to talk about this in mediation or talk to your solicitor prior to any court proceedings. There are a number of things that can be agreed as part of a parenting plan in these circumstances.

CHILDREN AT RISK

It is against the law to harm a child, and there are laws and policies to protect every child, even from members of their own family who are hurting them. These are called Child Protection Laws and Policies.

If you are worried that your partner is hurting your child/children, it is important for you to seek help. There are organisations that can help. Please see Chapter 7 for information on these organisations.

It is possible for the court to insist on supervised access, which is where a child only spends time with the parent in question when there is a trusted adult with them. This decision usually follows an assessment by the court to help it reach the right outcome.

The idea that you or your partner may have supervised or limited access to your children is very hard to face. There are no easy answers for anyone when a child is being harmed by one or both of their parents, or indeed when there is an accusation that this might be happening. The safety of the children is paramount and all you can do is be as honest as you can and seek good support.

TELLING THE EXTENDED FAMILY

When someone is bereaved, we can go to the funeral and sympathise. When a person is ill, we can visit them armed with bunches of grapes and kind words. However, as a society, we do not have good rituals for separation and divorce.

For the extended family of a separating couple, it can be a difficult time. Who do they support? What do they say? Do they keep in touch with the estranged in-law they used to be so fond of? Grandparents worry that they are not going to see their grandchildren. Cousins, aunts and uncles stop seeing each other as parents take sides.

As the couple themselves go through the tough reality of separation, the larger family are reeling from the effects. This time of separation is a process of family change. Relationships are redefined and expectations alter, and there is no roadmap to help everyone through.

Yet, when all is over and the agreement is in place, the family will still be there. Birthdays and weddings still need to be arranged and attended, and children still need the links with their extended family.

In reality, the extended family can be a help at this time if a few ground rules are put in place.

Try this...

1. When you are ready to tell your family, ask to meet them, sit down and tell them clearly that you and your partner are separating. You can decide whether to meet them together or separately, but do not leave it to someone else to do.

2. Be clear that your children need their support and, for their sake at least, you do not want your family to take sides against your partner, as your children love you both and it will be too hard for them.

3. Ask for their support but not their opinions, unless you specifically seek their advice. It can be too much pressure to have the people you care for pushing you one way or another.

4. Tell them that you and your partner are going to sort out the separation agreement between you and that you will let them know how it is going when you are ready. Ask them to respect your privacy.

WHAT IF OUR FAMILIES TAKE SIDES?

We cannot always account for how our two families respond to things that happen in our lives. Each family member has their own way of seeing things and of making their feelings heard, and it can be very difficult to stop things escalating.

What if a family member is constantly rude about and to your separating partner?

While you may agree with what your family member is saying, it can be very destructive to have someone you love constantly voicing their anger to your partner, particularly in front of your children and at a time when you are trying to negotiate a separation agreement. It can be a huge strain on top of everything else you are coping with.

Try this...

1. Ask to meet with the family member in a neutral venue.
2. Talk to them about how important their support is to you and how you appreciate the way they are feeling on your behalf.
3. Describe how their behaviour is affecting you and your children and the difficulties it is causing.
4. Ask them to help you by agreeing:
   a) Not to talk about your ex-partner in front of your children.
   b) To think about the effect it has on you and the children when a row starts at a family event.
   c) To try and keep any angry thoughts to themselves.

What if my partner and my family stop speaking to each other?

The breakdown of the relationship between your partner and your family is possibly the most common of inter-family difficulties. It can be particularly hard to adjust to if there was a tradition of good caring relationships beforehand. This really impacts on a family when it stops grandchildren spending time with grandparents.

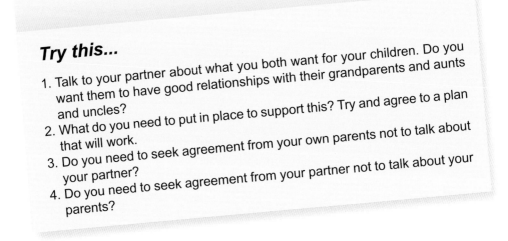

Try this...

1. Talk to your partner about what you both want for your children. Do you want them to have good relationships with their grandparents and aunts and uncles?
2. What do you need to put in place to support this? Try and agree to a plan that will work.
3. Do you need to seek agreement from your own parents not to talk about your partner?
4. Do you need to seek agreement from your partner not to talk about your parents?

If relationships become very bad, it is worth availing of the services of a mediator

Mediation is a conflict resolution process that can be used successfully in any type of conflict. It can be helpful to have a trained conflict resolution professional work with your family to help improve communication and help find a resolution.

What do I say to my partner's family?

There can be a lot of sadness when you are facing separation from your partner's family and, if we are honest, sometimes relief. Once the news of the separation is known, it can be so difficult to know what to say or how to act when meeting them in the street or at a family event.

There will be family members who you will still feel close to and others who you want to try and preserve a good working relationship with. It can be a good idea to use the same basic rules that you use with your own family.

Try this...

1. Ask to meet the person you are concerned about. Sit down and tell them clearly that you want to keep a good relationship with them. Do this as soon as you can after the news of your separation has become family knowledge. Do not leave this too long.

2. Tell them that you value your relationship with them and would like to try to keep things good between you. Promise that you will not talk about your partner or the separation to them and ask them to do the same. It can be too much pressure for both you.

3. Be clear that your children need their support and ask them to focus on keeping a good relationship with the children.

The people who care for you don't always know what to do for the best. They may need you to tell them how to support you. Grandparents of your children can be particularly worried.

TRAVELLING THE ROAD OF SEPARATION

As you set out to negotiate all the issues of separation, it is easy to become sidetracked by one issue or to return to the old fights of your relationship. When possible, keep your eyes ahead and focus on your future. Organise yourself so you can keep track of all the issues you have to deal with. This will help you feel more in control of events.

Try this...

When you got married, you planned it. Separation requires the same organisation. Think of this as a project.

1. Keep a file with all the documents and information you need.

2. Keep it away from the children.

3. Be careful about sending texts or e-mails in the heat of the moment.

4. Make sure you have support and downtime on the days when you have meetings.

5. Take responsibility for yourself and how you behave in meetings.

During your separation you will find that you will have to do things you have not done before. You might be very challenged by this, but if you take these challenges on you will be stronger at the end of the day.

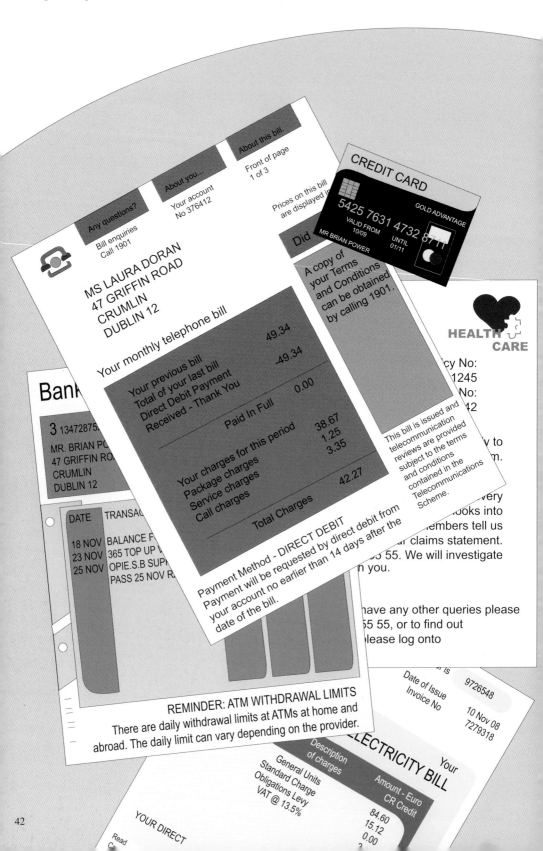

About this bill.

Front of page
1 of 3

Any questions?

Bill enquiries
Call 1901

About you...

Your account
No 376412

Prices on this bill
are displayed in

Did

A copy of
your Terms
and Conditions
can be obtained
by calling 1901.

CREDIT CARD

GOLD ADVANTAGE

5425 7631 4732 8711

VALID FROM
10/09

UNTIL
01/11

MR BRIAN POWER

HEALTH
CARE

MS LAURA DORAN
47 GRIFFIN ROAD
CRUMLIN
DUBLIN 12

cy No:
1245

No:
42

Your monthly telephone bill

This bill is issued and
telecommunication
reviews are provided
subject to the terms
and conditions
contained in the
Telecommunications
Scheme.

y to
m.

Your previous bill   49.34

Total of your last bill   -49.34

Direct Debit Payment
Received - Thank You   0.00

Paid In Full

Your charges for this period   38.67
Package charges   1.25
Service charges   3.35
Call charges

Total Charges   42.27

very
ooks into
embers tell us
claims statement.
55. We will investigate
h you.

Bank

3 13472875

MR. BRIAN PO
47 GRIFFIN RO
CRUMLIN
DUBLIN 12

DATE   TRANSAC

18 NOV   BALANCE F
23 NOV   365 TOP UP
25 NOV   OPIE.S.B SUPF
         PASS 25 NOV R

Payment Method - DIRECT DEBIT
Payment will be requested by direct debit from
your account no earlier than 14 days after the
date of the bill.

have any other queries please
55 55, or to find out
lease log onto

REMINDER: ATM WITHDRAWAL LIMITS
There are daily withdrawal limits at ATMs at home and
abroad. The daily limit can vary depending on the provider.

Date of Issue   9726548
Invoice No

                       10 Nov 08
                       7279318

ELECTRICITY BILL   Your

Description
of charges

General Units
Standard Charge
Obligations Levy
VAT @ 13.5%

Amount - Euro
CR Credit

84.60
15.12
0.00

YOUR DIRECT

Read

42

FINANCE

The most important thing when it comes to the budget for your family is that you have enough money to run two homes.

Money

Money can be at the heart of so many rows in families and can be a very big worry at a time of separation. Who is responsible for what? Will there be enough? How can we trust what the other person is saying?

How to manage money in separation

Although you are separating, the joint income that has covered the needs of the family in one home is still the joint income that will be used to cover the cost of two homes, unless there is a way to earn more.

If your figures do not add up then it will be very difficult to agree on maintenance.

What is maintenance?

Maintenance is the name given to the amount of money agreed between you to maintain each other and any children, in accordance with the money available.

There are two types of maintenance:

> **Spousal:** spousal maintenance is for the needs of the spouse.

> **Child:** child maintenance is for the needs of the children.

HOW DO WE WORK OUT WHAT IS FAIR?

Establish the facts about money.

Step 1: Information

You will need to gather information and details of the following:

What you earn:
      a) Your most recent P60 and three recent pay slips.
      b) If you are self-employed, annual accounts for the past three years.
      c) Social welfare details.

What you own:
      a) Insurance policy details plus surrender values.
      b) Details of any savings, e.g. credit union book, etc.
      c) Pension scheme: you will need your explanatory booklet plus any recent benefits statements.

What you owe:
You will need details of both joint and personal debt.

When you start mediation or go to your solicitor, they will ask you for this information, so keep hold of it. It also contains a lot of the information you will need for the next step. Make sure your information is up-to-date and accurate.

Step 2: Work out how you, as a separated family, will spend your money

You can download a sample budget sheet from our website www.livingwithseparation.com. Each of you need to work out your expenses as individuals. Base your expenditure figures on what you believe your expenses will be when you live in two separate places.

Then link both lists together to get the overall running costs for each of you and your children. Until you have these figures you cannot come to an agreement that will last into the future.

You will have to make an educated guess at some of the figures, but this exercise will help you get to grips with the budget. You may not have decided where each of you will live, so estimate the cost of a second property for the purpose of the exercise.

Download a budget sheet at www.livingwithseparation.com

Step 3: Joint cost

Add both of your final expenditure figures together. This will give you a total figure for what it will cost to run both homes.

Step 4: Joint income

Write down all your income and add it together.

Step 5: Balancing the budget

Which figure is bigger?

Joint Expenditure   €XXXX

Joint Income   €XXXX

     - €XXXX

Difference

If the expenditure is bigger than the income then you will have to look at balancing the budget:

     a) What are necessary expenses?
     b) What can you cut back on?
     c) Is there any way of earning extra money?

You may find that the projected monthly deficit is similar to the cost of a second home.

Step 6: How do we work out child maintenance?

You will have included child expenses in the budget. How much do they come to?

You will also need to account for housing, food, utilities and transport expenses.

Focus on these questions:
- What do we want for our children?
- How can we use our income to give them the quality of life we want for them?
- How do we organise our money so that it does not cause rows between us?

It is important to understand the different taxation options that you have when you separate. You may need to seek specialist tax advice before making a final financial decision.

TAX

Your tax will change when you separate or divorce, as you are changing from being taxed as a married couple to being taxed as two single persons. You will find that some of the decisions you make will have different tax implications.

For example, when there is an agreement for one of you to provide payments such as spousal maintenance or child maintenance there may be a difference in how each of these are taxed. In some countries:

- If the payment is child maintenance, it is ignored for tax purposes. The partner who makes the payment does not have a tax deduction for it and the spouse receiving the payment is not taxed on it.

- If the payment is spousal maintenance, it is taxable for the receiving spouse. The paying spouse does not pay tax on it.

Each country has its own tax system so it is important to seek the information relevant to your situation before making your final decision.

ASSETS

The first thing you need to do is to create a complete list of assets, which you own both jointly and separately.

These will include:

1. Other properties such as houses, apartments and land.
2. Parts of properties you may own with other people.
3. Contents of the family home.
4. Boats, caravans, mobile homes, etc.
5. A company or business.
6. Share certificates.
7. Credit union books and deposit account books.
8. Life assurance policies.
9. Pensions.

It is worth taking the time to collect the documentation and up-to-date valuations into a folder, as you will need these for your agreement.

Valuing assets such as a company or business can be a complex job. You may need to take professional advice on how to do this. Deciding what to do about dividing such an asset can be particularly difficult, if the same business is providing an income for one or both or you.

What if my partner decides to hide some of their assets?

If you are unsure that you are getting a complete list from your partner and you are in either mediation or with a solicitor, raise this with them when you are at a meeting. If there is not full disclosure of all assets, a legal search can be done.

If you are married, all assets are considered marital assets and have to be declared at the time of separation.

How do we decide how to divide our assets?

Quite often the division of assets will happen as part of the overall negotiation of your separation. There are, however, assets that will be particularly yours or your partner's, such as cars, jewelry or possessions with sentimental value. You may find you can come to an informal agreement about these.

What about the contents of the family home?

The easiest way of dealing with the contents of the family home is to make a list that both of you agree on and then put ticks beside who is going to take what article. Sometimes couples come to an agreement that whoever moves out of the home and needs to furnish a new place will have a small amount of money from the joint savings to pay for cookers, fridges, beds, etc.

Contents of the home can also be negotiated as part of your overall agreement, but it can sometimes be easier to agree the list between you.

DEBT

As with assets, the first thing you need to do is to create a list of all of the family debt. This will include:

1. Mortgages on the family home and other properties.
2. Bank loans (car, personal, etc.).
3. Credit union loans.
4. Credit card debt.
5. Overdrafts.

All debt will have to be either paid off as part of your agreement or divided between you, taking into account who has the ability to pay back what debt.

If you are married, all debt is considered marital debt and needs to be dealt with at the time of separation.

It can be very difficult to work out who is responsible for the actual debt accrued in a relationship. Credit cards are used for family expenditure. One of you may have taken out a loan for household needs. There could be quite a few arguments before this area is finalised.

It is important to agree a package that each of you can manage. Without this balance, one of you will struggle and begin to get behind with payments and this could have a knock-on effect on other financial arrangements, particularly if there are children involved.

PENSIONS

Pensions can be one of the most valuable assets you have to make a decision about in your separation. Most people start paying into a pension when they start work and it grows over the years. At the time of retirement, the money saved up in the pension is released according to the terms of the pension fund. This might mean that you get a lump sum of money and then regular payments every week or month.

If you get married, then your spouse has the right to a percentage of your pension for every year that you were married. At the time of divorce, a decision will have to be made as to what to do with this entitlement as it is an asset which will have to be divided.

What about the State pension?

Some people may be entitled to a pension from the State when they reach a certain age. However, a State pension may not be adequate to provide for more than the bare essentials in old age. It is important to think about how to provide for your later years when negotiating your separation or divorce.

What most working people do

Most working people contribute during the course of their working lives to a pension scheme through their employer, or voluntarily through private pension arrangements if they are self-employed.

This means that, over time, a person may end up with several pension plans, over and above any State pension entitlements they might have.

The process

Your pension is included in the family assets. It does not matter which one of you is the member of the pension scheme; it is seen as a family asset.

There are clear legal guidelines on how family pensions are divided. Any informal agreement you may come to will not be valid unless you have a **Pension Adjustment Order (PAO)**. The trustees of the pension scheme can only carry out your agreement if there is a valid PAO in place. This type of order is sought by going through the courts.

It is legally and morally important for each of you to be completely open and transparent with regard to providing details of pensions and entitlements from employed or self-employed sources, present and past.

Please note: Sometimes, as part of an overall agreement, a court will decide that a PAO is not needed. There may be some other way of providing fairly for each of you in your old age without tampering with the pension schemes themselves. It is important, before going to court on this issue, that you take good pension and legal advice.

What do I need to know?

The most important question that you will be asked is: What is your pension worth at the point when you and your partner separate or divorce?

How do I work this out?

Generally there are two types of pension plans:

Defined contribution: Where you will be given a complete or capital value of your pension plan every year. In the document there will be a figure telling you how much your total pension is worth at this time. This is the figure you need.

Defined benefit: You will be given information on what you will get at the time you retire. You will not have a figure for what the capital value is at this time. If you need to find out this figure, you will need to go to an actuary and ask them to give you the capital value of your pension.

What are the questions that we need to ask ourselves?

A pension is designed to give you financial security in your old age. It can also be worth a lot of money and can be key in negotiating a balanced separation agreement. Here are some important questions:

1. Does one of you have a much bigger pension, or more pensions, than the other?
2. If so, how can you balance this so that you both have security in your old age?
3. Do you have other big assets worth a similar amount to the pensions?
4. If so, can you use these to negotiate a balanced and fair deal?

What will happen if we are dealing with our separation in court?

The court will make their ruling on pensions based on the following:

1. How long you have been married.
2. Proper provision for all of the spouses and children, taking into account all of their assets, their liabilities and their income. It may not decide a 50/50 split; this will depend on the overall picture.

Before you put a proposal in front of the court, it will be better for you to take good advice from a pension expert. There may be a number of options for you and you need to consider all the options and consequences before you present your case.

Decisions

Pensions can be among the most valuable assets you have to make a decision about in your separation.

The life insurance industry has standard methods, approved by Revenue, for working out the capital value of a pension.

Rules

There are a number of rigidly enforced rules, regulations and laws that apply to pensions. The reason for this is, as well as there being valuable tax incentives for building up pension funds, pensions need to be kept safe from potential fraud and misappropriation. They can also include valuable death benefits for spouses and dependent children.

They are of vital importance to any family's future security.

The rules in your pension scheme will probably include:

- **You do not legally own your pension fund**. It is the legal property of the pension scheme trustees, who own the pension fund on your behalf. There will be a legal record and contract to this effect. This is regulated under law and there are no exceptions.

- With some minor and clear exceptions, **once money is put into a pension scheme it will not be returned to you until you reach retirement age**, as laid down in the pension scheme rules.

- **The rules of the pension scheme, which have the force of law, will clearly**

lay down how the money can be paid out to you in retirement. Not all schemes have the same payout rules.

The various family and pension laws rule very clearly on pensions as important family assets and on the entitlements of spouses and dependants to their legitimate part of family pension benefits.

What information do we need?

You will need:

- Name, address and contact details of all employers (including those overseas) up to the present date, through which you or your spouse may have contributed to an occupational pension scheme or other group scheme and not taken back your contributions or transferred any pension benefits elsewhere.

- Dates of employment (accurate) with employers in the above list.

- Copy of the scheme explanatory booklet (rules) for each scheme on your list of employers.

- List of any private or self-employed pension plans, past and present.

- Details of the underwriters of any private or self-employed pension plans (for example, Irish Life, New Ireland, Aviva, etc.).

- Most recent benefit statements from all pension plans from the lists above. If any of the benefit statements are more than one year old, or if you can't find particular benefit statements, you will need to ask the employer, ex-employer or underwriter to send you an up-to-date benefit statement. No meaningful progress can be made without these.

- If you don't have scheme explanatory booklets from each employer, you will need to ask for this too. You can't proceed properly without it.

All this information is vital to making good decisions about your future pension needs. If you do not have all of this, it is worth taking the time to track it down. A lot of money can be lost if you enter legal proceedings without all the paperwork being prepared.

Dealing with pensions under the circumstances of separation can be difficult and confusing. It is worth taking your time and doing it right. Take professional advice and do not leave things undecided.

How do we make a decision about our pensions?

When you have had a qualified professional provide you with a guide on the capital value of the family pension plan or plans, and any other factors or conditions you should be aware of such as death benefits, you can use this in conjunction with the value of other family assets, for example, property, to negotiate an acceptable overall settlement, depending on your particular financial needs and requirements.

You may decide to split pensions by way of a PAO or you may not, depending on what is acceptable to both you and your spouse. Either way, it is in your own financial interests to take proper account of all values and conditions in the light of your existing and expected circumstances.

It may be very hard and stressful work, but if you and your spouse can reach a fair and balanced settlement, it will be hugely beneficial to you, your spouse and any children, emotionally and financially. The agreement will then need to be sanctioned with the necessary decrees and orders through the courts. This is not a contentious process and will normally be carried out by instructing your solicitor.

If you cannot agree an acceptable settlement, your choices are to leave things as they are, or to start contentious legal proceedings, as explained below.

What if we cannot agree a fair and balanced settlement?

Unless you decide just to leave things as they are, you will normally then appoint a solicitor to issue legal proceedings and formally present your case to the courts. Of course, this is a contentious process and will be contested by your spouse's legal advisors.

From the information presented and the pleadings made by each side, the courts will then decide how the assets will be split, including pensions. You will, of course, have gone into this process with all the correct pension information to hand in the first place. That will help you focus on a desirable outcome and will reduce the potential for unnecessary delays, frustration, stress and expense due to incomplete or inaccurate pension information.

The courts have complete discretion on how to split the assets, including pensions, having regard to the facts and circumstances of the particular case. It would be unwise to try to predict exactly how it might decide, but you should follow the advice of a specialised and experienced family law solicitor.

In conclusion

Take professional advice, and, as regards sorting the pension element in a separation, do it right or don't do it at all, as you will only end up paying far more than you should to achieve a resolution.

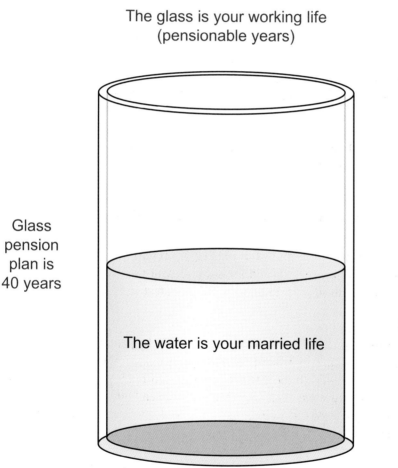

The glass is your working life
(pensionable years)

Glass
pension
plan is
40 years

The water is your married life

20 years
of water
in the
glass

The court will normally look at
half the water in the glass

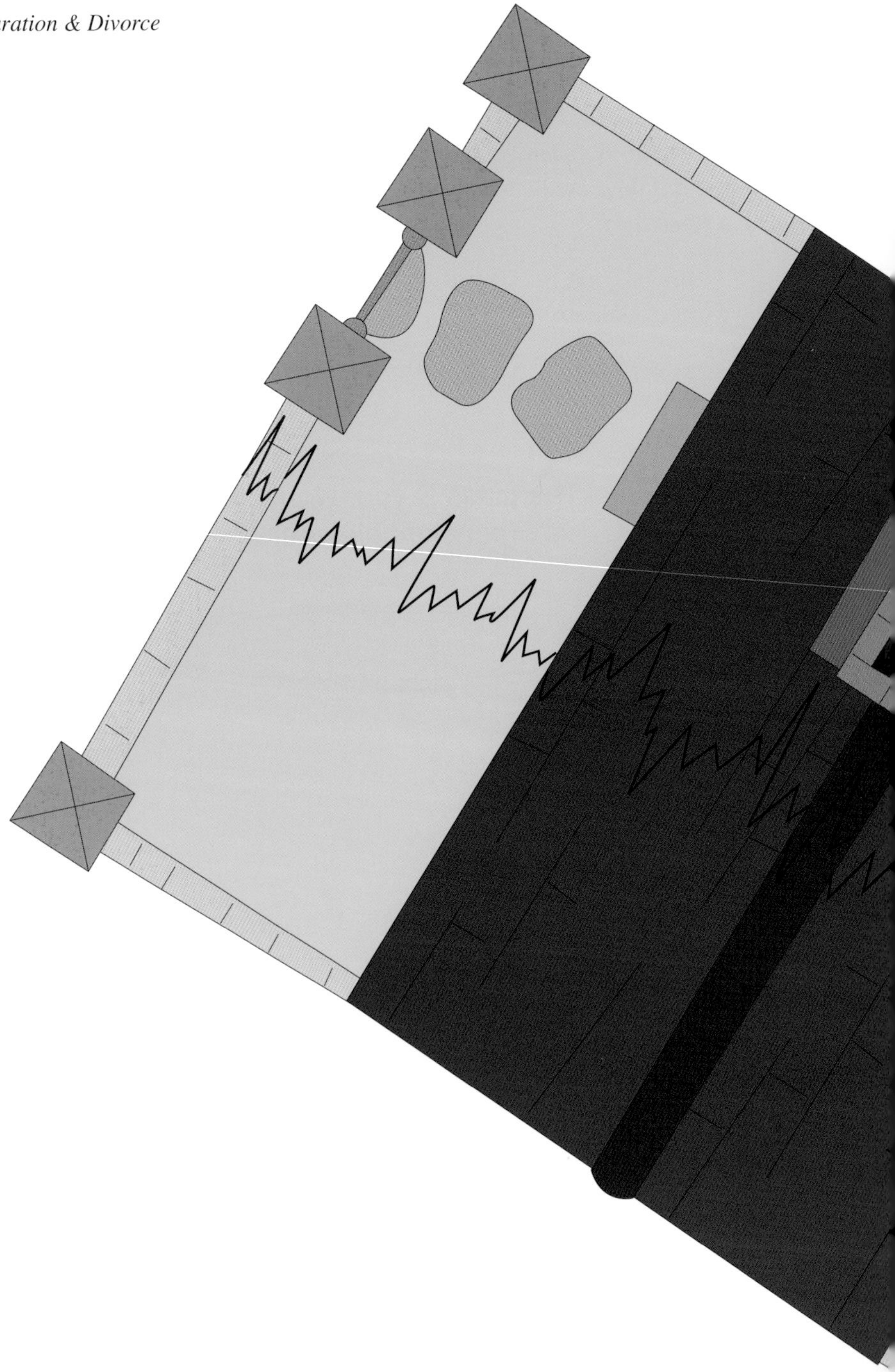

(3)

FAMILY HOME

The home is where, generally, our heart is. The first few years of living together are often filled with the excitement and anxieties of buying, furnishing and doing up the place we want to stay, put down roots and raise our family. It is a bitter blow to lose, not only the dreams of a happy marriage, but also the roof over our heads.

So, how is it possible to quantify the value of the home we live in? Is it as simple as going and getting a valuation from the local estate agent? Is it better to fight it out in court and have someone else decide?

The family home can be most couples' biggest financial asset, so a good decision has to be made. But perhaps the real value of any home is the happiness it brings to the lives of those within.

Try this...

1. List what you think you need in a new home.
2. Go through the list and mark what is essential and what is less essential.
3. Make a note of what you would be willing to forego, if you had to.
4. Keep the list as a checklist of what is important to you. If you get caught up in a row over the family home, go back to this list to remind you what you are aiming for.

The value of any home is subjective. It can be different for each individual.

Agreeing on how to value your property and accepting the result will help you reach a fairer outcome.

THE VALUATION OF THE FAMILY HOME

It is not unusual for each of you to have a different idea of how much the home is worth. This can be influenced by what you want to happen to the home.

It is probably fair to accept that neither of you have a totally objective view of the value, and that asking for and accepting a professional valuation may be the best way forward.

Here are some ideas:

1. Agree on three different valuers to value the property and settle on the middle valuation.

or

2. Agree on a valuer you both trust and agree that you will accept their valuation.

CHOICES IN RELATION TO THE FAMILY HOME

There is a number of basic options regarding the family home in cases of separation. Whether decided by a court or agreed between the couple, one of the following options will apply:

Selling the family home

This tends to be the option chosen by couples with no children or whose children have grown up. The steps are as follows:

1. Engage an estate agent.
2. Agree a valuation and reserve price (see section on valuation of family home).
3. Agree a date for the home to go onto the market.
4. Agree how to divide the equity.

Buying out the family home

This tends to be the choice couples prefer, if there are children. It means that one parent has a secure home with the children and the other has money to go and create their own home for themselves and their children.

The steps are as follows:

1. A buy-out involves paying off the original mortgage plus giving a percentage of the remaining equity in the home to the other party, ie:

Existing mortgage + cash buy-out = complete buy-out

2. If the mortgage is the same as the equity in the home then there is no cash buy-out.

3. Find out what the person doing the buying out can get from a lender. Is this enough to pay off the mortgage and pay a fair amount to the other to start again?

4. If so, this can be the basis for an agreement.

Signing over the family home

Occasionally couples decide that one will sign over the home to the other. This often happens where there are other assets to offset the value of the equity in the home, or if there is a mortgage which is the same as the value of the property and therefore there is no actual value to be shared.

Deferring a decision on the family home

This decision tends to be one made by couples with young children. They would like the children to stay in the family home and grow up there. Usually the main carer, often the mother, would live in the family home with the children and the other parent would move out. There are a number of factors to consider:

1. How long will this arrangement be in place?
2. What will happen at the end of this time?
3. Who will be in charge of paying the mortgage?
4. If you are sharing the payment of this, how will this work in practice?
5. How will the parent living in the family home manage their privacy?

Nesting

This is an arrangement that couples will agree to in order to leave their children in the family home full time. Each parent finds somewhere else to live then spends scheduled time in the family home with the children. Mum and Dad "fly in and out the nest" where their children reside.

The schedule needs to be well managed and the couple need to be able to communicate well and accommodate each other. The advantage is that the children do not have to move from home to home.

Negative equity

In some cases, the value of the family home can be less than the mortgage. This is called negative equity. If this is the case, the bank or lender who holds the mortgage may need to be involved in the decision about the family home. It is important to contact them as soon as you can.

WHEN CHILDREN ARE INVOLVED...
...THE REAL PICTURE

A family home is paid for with a combination of cash and a mortgage

Mortgage
covers the difference between the equity and the value of the home

% of Cash/Equity
from existing family home is required to pay for children's main place of residence

Children's main place of residence

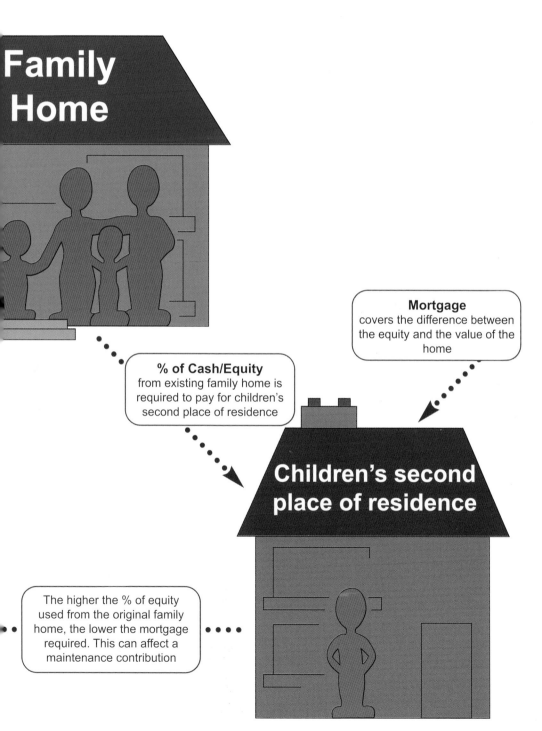

FAIRNESS

So, how will you know what is fair and whether you have been fair to each other?

Fairness is something we each define differently and, as you negotiate your separation, this will be a central issue for you. When you divide the contents of the family home, and as you look at the issues for asset division and debt payment, this question of fairness will run all the way through.

It is easy to argue about your rights but it is better to negotiate a fair deal that lets you both move on.

When it comes to the family home, settling on a fair chance at a happy future in a home in which you can start again is a good focus.

Look at the diagram on the previous page. Both parents have an obligation to pay towards the housing needs of their children, either through putting equity into the home or contributing towards a mortgage.

If there is more equity going into the new family home for the children, or remaining in the family home already there, then mortgage repayments will be less. In turn, that can mean the maintenance paid by the other parent could be less. If there is less equity, then the resulting bigger mortgage could lead to a need for bigger maintenance payments.

WHEN ONE OF YOU CARRIES ON LIVING IN THE FAMILY HOME

If one of you is staying in the family home and the other is going back and forth picking up and dropping children off, then it is important to agree some ground rules.

The person living in the home will need some privacy and it may be a good idea to arrange for the one living away from the home not to have a key anymore. If a key is retained, then agree to have some parts of the house private.

Agreeing basic rules at the start can make things easier down the line.

Children most often cite the hand-over between their parents as the most stressful time for them. Often parents talk about how their children cry when they are being dropped back to or picked up from the family home. This can be because of the parents' behaviour towards each other.

Children also worry about what the parent who has left the family home will do. They want to see them happy and safe with a nice home too.

Try this...

1. Take the children to see the new home. Be positive for your children, even if it is hard.
2. Make sure there are pictures of each parent in the other parent's home (maybe in the children's bedroom) so that the children feel at home in both places.
3. Discuss how to make the hand-over time as easy for the children as possible. Stick to the agreement.
4. This is a time of adjustment for everyone. Agree to talk about any issues between you concerning the family home at a different time from the hand-over of the children.
5. Accept that this is going to be hard for each of you in different ways.

YOUR CHILDREN

What do we do about the kids?
I never wanted this for them!
How will I hand them over to him to look after?
What if they need me?
I'm going to be a single mum!
Does he understand what they need like I do?
I am worried!
I feel guilty!
I love my kids!
I am going to fight for them!
The kids come first...

What do we do about the kids?
How will I wake up in the morning and not see my children?
I won't be able to tuck them in at night.
Why shouldn't I have the children?
Isn't a father just as important as the mother?
It's not my fault I have to work long hours.
I am going to miss them.
I love my kids!
I need to fight for them!
The kids come first...

TELLING THE CHILDREN

Telling the children about the separation is one of the most difficult things for couples to face. How and when to do it and what to say can be considerable worries. Parents worry about getting these things right and how they themselves are going to cope when they start talking to their children.

It is very important for parents to tell children as clearly and honestly as they can. At the end of the day, the fact that you are separating cannot be erased or wished away for your child. Parents cannot ignore the fact that they have to help their child face this huge family change and that this will take time.

It is not possible to shelter children from the effects of separation, but it is possible to find positive ways to help them deal with it.

Key needs for children during separation:

- Clear explanations from their parents about what is happening.
- Good relationships with both parents during and after separation.
- Parents who can recognise and respond to their needs.
- Not to have to choose between their parents.

What children need to hear:

- Mum and Dad are not happy together anymore and have decided to live apart.
- We are still your mum and dad and will take care of you.
- What has happened between us is not your fault.
- The separation is permanent. We will not change our minds.
- Nothing will ever change the fact that we both love you.
- We are still your parents and will decide a future plan for our family. We will tell you the moment we have agreed what we are going to do.
- We love you and you can talk to us anytime.
- We will try and answer any questions you have as honestly as we can.

Most children say that they would have liked to know sooner about their parents' separation.

How to tell them:

1. As soon as the separation has become a firm decision between you, it is time to focus on telling your children.

2. It is important to talk and plan beforehand what you will say and how you will say it.

3. If possible, both parents should tell the child/children together.

4. Try and leave any feelings of anger, blame or guilt you have towards each other to one side. Children do not do well when they are in the middle of parents who are arguing.

5. Children need to hear clearly that you are separating, you love them and are still there for them, and that it is not their fault.

6. Leave time over the following days to talk to your children and listen to their questions. It can take time for children to process what is happening and they may need to go over it many times.

7. Your children will react in different ways. They may cry, or get very angry. On the other hand, they may say nothing and become withdrawn. Be patient and remember that the time you give to your children now is hugely helpful to them.

8. Tell them it is alright to be upset and that you are both there for them whenever they need you.

How to support them:

1. Children look to their parents for comfort and support. If they see Mum and Dad being positive, they feel better themselves. Remember to tell your children that you love them and that you will be there for them throughout this difficult process of family change. Be optimistic.

2. Maintain as much continuity and routine as possible for the children. Keep friendships and school attendance going, and carry on with your child's usual activities. A child who feels secure and positive about themselves will cope better with the separation.

3. Keep your child informed about what is happening and why. It is important for children to know that you are listening to their wishes and feelings.

However, do remember that they will find it difficult if they are asked to make decisions regarding parenting arrangements which may involve choosing between parents.

4.   Encourage other family members on both sides of the family, who have good relationships with your children, to be involved in their lives.

5.   Resist the temptation to make up for your child's loss with material things or lack of discipline in the home. Emotional hurt is best healed with care, support and consistency in parenting, not things.

6.   Encourage your children to join a peer support programme. Children can find it helpful to meet other children who have had similar experiences. It helps them feel less lonely.

7.   Let all significant adults in your child's life know about the separation so that they can help support the children.

PARENTING TOGETHER

Parenting your children will not be the same after separation. You will each have times when your children are not with you and you will both experience the feeling of loss. There is no way that this can be avoided so it is better to acknowledge it up front.

There will be many feelings competing for your attention at this time:

- It may be that you want to hold on to what you have, feeling that any diminishment of your time with the children is tantamount to a loss of power.

- You may feel that the other parent does not understand your concerns for the children and thinks that you are "getting your own back" through them.

- The idea of your children sleeping in a different house from you may be too much to bear.

Whatever your feelings are, there is no doubt that everyone in the family feels anxious and everyone in the family is vulnerable. Children at this time also feel worried about their future and what might happen, and bereft at losing time with either parent. The difference for them is that all too often they are in the middle of the rows and fights, and, even when there are no rows, they feel that they may have to choose between their parents... an impossible choice for any child.

It is therefore of considerable importance that, whatever you feel, you are able to see through these feelings and endeavour to put your children's needs first.

Children do not want any other parents other than the ones they have.
>They love you and they want you to look after them.
>This is their first and foremost wish.
>They are both resilient and vulnerable.
>They can cope but need your care.

Shared parenting is often put forward as the best plan for your children, but is it possible for you and your separated partner to do this?

Try answering these:

1. When you were together, did you share the parenting of your children?
2. If not, is there a commitment to do so now?
3. Can you communicate fairly well about your children?
4. Can you make joint decisions on their behalf?
5. Do you have a basic respect for your ex-partner as a parent?
6. Can you put your own disagreements to one side and concentrate on your children?
7. Can you allow each other to parent in your own style?
8. Can you work out which differences between your parenting styles are important and which are not?
9. Do you value what the other parent has to offer your children?
10. Are you willing to cope with the extra work involved in the parenting plan?

How do you think your children would answer these questions?
How might their answers differ from yours?

IT IS NEVER TOO LATE

Take time to look ahead

What do you want your children to say about their parents when they are young adults?

"My mum and dad split up when I was young and they..."

How do you want that sentence to finish?

This can be quite a challenging thing to think about, but it can also be a helpful focus for you as you think about what is important for your children at this time.

How we behave as parents is one of the biggest influences our children have in their lives. They are fundamentally affected by what they experience through us. What do you want your children to learn from this experience they are going through now? You can do a lot to influence this answer by how you and your partner behave.

If children are continuously in the middle of rows then they are learning that every problem leads to an argument, that disagreeing means calling the other person names and raising your voice. They are seeing that other people's opinions don't merit respect and that it is okay to be dishonest or to withhold information from one another.

You may have been arguing for years and are fearful of what the children have seen and heard. This may worry you and you might feel that it is too late. Well, it is never too late to change and your children will then learn that resolution is always possible, no matter how serious the conflict.

When you argue, your child is torn in two. Try and keep the worst of the arguing away from them.

It can be an important life lesson to learn that, even when a situation has been very bad, it is possible to turn things around; that, even when arguments are really fierce, it is possible to make some sort of peace at the end of the day.

It is never too late to change and, as you work your way through your separation and settle into your new life, it will feel easier.

Try this...

Answer these questions:

1. How much quality time do you spend with your children?

2. Has your parenting been consumed by the conflict between you?

3. How has this conflict changed you and stopped you being the parent you want to be?

4. What would you like to change?

5. Can you make those changes?

6. If you asked your children what they would like to change, what do you think they would say?

NEW PARTNERS

The arrival of a new partner can be highly controversial for parents, particularly if it is someone that one of you met prior to the separation. If this is particularly difficult for you, it is worth using the services of a mediator to help discuss and agree how you handle this issue as a couple.

Your children will never want to replace either of you as parents. They will not see a new partner as a potential parent. They, however, can develop good relationships with the new partner, if a few simple agreements are observed. While this may be a very difficult thing to accept, it is healthier for your children to get along with this new friend in their parent's life.

If children are left to figure out what is going on by themselves, knowing that they upset one parent by being in the same room as the other parent's partner or wondering who this new person is who is suddenly in their lives, they can soon become distressed and confused. The parenting arrangements that had been working well start to run into problems as the children struggle to cope with what to think or do.

Try this...

1. Agree that for a period of six months after you separate neither of you will introduce new partners to your children. This helps the children to get used to the separation first.
2. Agree that, as part of the separation, you accept your ex-partner's right to a private life.
3. Agree as part of the separation that you both understand the need for your children to spend time with each of you alone.
4. Be prepared to talk about the parenting implications of new people coming into your lives. It can be a hard conversation to have but it is better to have some idea of what you both think, rather than waiting until it happens.
5. If you have met someone significant and you do want them to meet your children, talk to the other parent first. Your children will get along with this new person in their lives a lot better if they know the other parent is, or seems, okay with it.
6. Do not do this the night before the planned introduction, as this will create unnecessary tension for the other parent and your children.
7. Do leave time for several conversations with your separated partner about this, so that all parenting issues have been dealt with by the time the introduction has taken place.
8. If one of you plans to move in with a new partner, arrange to meet to discuss and agree any changes to the parenting plan that will be necessary.

PARENTING PLAN

A parenting plan is part of the separation agreement or divorce that sets out how you will parent your children. It covers guardianship, custody and access, which are the legal terms, respectively, for:

1. Who is responsible for caring for your children: If you are married you are already joint guardians and jointly responsible for making decisions on your children's health, education and welfare. In some countries there are different legal rules for when parents are not married.

2. Who your children live with: Children often have a main place of residence with one parent, and time, including overnights, with the other. Some parents share the time equally between them. It is important for the children to have a place where they formally reside and where any mail addressed to them goes.

3. When they spend time with each of you: There needs to be a clear week-by-week schedule so that everyone knows who is staying with who and on what day.

It can be very helpful to have a parenting plan. This is a clear schedule outlining when the children are with each parent and can also include holiday arrangements and care plans.

Here is an simple example:

	Monday	Tuesday	Wednesday	Thursday	Friday	Saturday	Sunday
Week 1	M	D	D	M	M	D	M
Week 2	M	M	M	D	M	D	D
Week 3	M	D	D	M	M	D	M
Week 4	M	M	M	D	M	D	D

Mum = M

Dad = D

How do we make a parenting plan?

NOBODY LOVES YOUR CHILDREN LIKE YOU DO.
NOBODY CAN MAKE CHOICES FOR THEM THE WAY YOU CAN.

Parenting plans are often decided by a judge in court. However, you and your separating partner are the people that know your children best and you are the ones who will be living by this plan. It will be down to you to make this work.

Research shows that, if parents negotiate their own plan, they are more than likely to stick to it.

It is possible to go to mediation to negotiate parenting arrangements. However, here are some ideas of how to do it yourself:

1. Arrange a time when you are both able to sit down and talk.

2. Bring a calendar so you can view the weeks, months and full year.

3. Bring a notebook so you can keep notes of your agreement (not to keep tabs on each other!).

4. Bring photos of your children and put them on the table. If you slip into an argument, look at the photos. Think of what your children would say to you right now. Remind yourselves that your children love you both. Take three deep breaths and start again.

5. Use the template in this book (previous page) as a guide.

6. Think about what the children would want. Reading this chapter should be helpful.

Consider the following:

Residence:
- Will the children have one primary residence or two?
- When will they stay with each parent and for how long?

Holidays:
- How will major school holidays be shared?
- How will vacations be agreed on?

Christmas:
- How will you share Christmas?
- Will you alternate?
- Can you come together for some time on the day itself?
- Do the children have two Christmas Days (24th, 25th and 26th shared).

Financial Support:
- How do you pay for the needs of your children?
- What are the needs of your children per month? (download budget sheet from www.livingwithseparation.com)
- Do you need to create an account for future educational, medical, etc. needs?
- How will child care be paid for?

Routine Care:
- Who will oversee the medical/dental needs of the children?
- Who will be responsible for school homework, activities, transport?
- Who will be responsible for arranging child care?

Authority for Decision Making:
- How will decisions be made?
- What areas need joint decision making?
- Do you need to make a list of these areas?

Legal Custody:
- Will you have joint, split or sole custody?

Disagreements:
- How will you handle large disagreements?
- Is it a good idea to agree to go to a mediator when there is a dispute?

THROUGH YOUR CHILDREN'S EYES

Children are often the first to realise that things are wrong between their parents. They may not actually know what is happening but they live right in the midst of the breakdown. Every day they experience the rows and the silences, the ups and the downs of a relationship coming to an end, and will quite often wonder and worry long before they are actually told about the separation. Many children say that they wished their parents had told them sooner about the separation.

When they eventually do hear, the emotional impact on the children, however expected, is considerable. It is important for parents to be aware that, as well as being clear in the information they give to their children, they will have to support them through some difficult emotions.

Children need to talk about how they feel. They may feel:

Angry: At Mum and Dad for doing this to them.

Anxious: About the future.

Relieved: That, when they are told, at last they know what is going on.

Sad: Quite often children want to cry and cry when they are told.

Confused: At what they feel and how to react.

Bereft: At the loss of their family as they know it.

Guilty: Because they believe it is their fault.

Children will cope best if both parents cooperate with each other, rebuilding their lives and working to resolve any problems together.

DIFFERENT STAGES OF CHILDHOOD

How children cope with separation will depend on their age. Developing a plan for children according to their ages means that certain aspects need to be taken into account for each age group.

INFANT AND TODDLER

I bond with my parents through their care and play.

I need to see each parent regularly.

I need both parents to know how to look after me.

I need a regular routine that does not change from day to day.

I learn to feel safe through a stable routine.

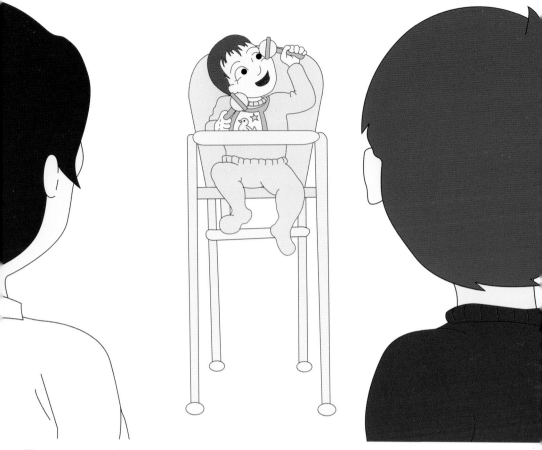

- The parenting schedule should include regular time with both parents.

- If one parent has not been caring for the child on a daily basis, these regular times should be for a few hours to begin with and include learning the baby's routine. As things develop, overnights can then be included.

- If both parents are in the habit of caring for the child then overnights should be included from the start.

- The baby's routine must be kept consistent in both parents' houses. This is what they need to feel secure.

- If there is one principal carer, then one overnight a week plus a few hours three or four times a week for the other parent can work well. As the child grows to be a toddler, full weekends with the other parent can be included.

- If child care is in place, it is better to keep the same child minder.

- Concentrate on your child while you are with them. Be there for them, listen and interact. Minimise the time you spend on your mobile phone.

PRE-SCHOOL: 4–5

I want my independence!

I am working out what it means to be a girl or boy.

I need time with both my parents to help me do this.

I need lots of reassurance that they love me.

I worry about being abandoned.

I have no concept of time and get anxious when I don't see one parent for a long time.

- Work hard to keep good communication.

- Use a notebook to write down information. This can be handed back and forth between you and cuts down the need for long conversations at the hand-over times.

  - If you are sharing the parenting, think in terms of 3-4 day blocks when working out the schedule.
  - Keep the routine consistent.
  - Use a calendar to mark the days so the child can understand the schedule.

- If one parent has been the principal care giver, then build up the time away from this parent gradually. Maybe one night at the weekend and one mid-week would be good to start with.

- Both parents should try to go to pre-school events.

- Concentrate on your child while you are with them. Be there for them, listen and interact. Minimise the time you spend on your mobile phone.

SCHOOL AGE: 6–12 YEARS

I have friends and my own world of school and play.

I would rather stay in my own neighbourhood and play.

I want things to be fair.

I can become very angry with the parent who I think has been unfair.

I can worry about the parent I feel is lonely or sad.

I can take on the responsibility of trying to make things better between my parents, which is not good for me.

If I am a boy, I need to know that I will be having regular time with my dad. I can feel very sad.

- Work hard to keep good communication.

- Use a notebook to write down information. This can be handed back and forth between you and cuts down the need for long conversations at the hand-over times.

- Take time to organise the two homes so that the children don't constantly worry about not having the right books or clothes for school.

- Reassure your children that you are both working to make things fair and they do not need to worry.

- Reassure them that, if there is a problem, you and the other parent will sort it out.

- Try and help your children keep good consistent friendships.

- Concentrate on your child while you are with them. Be there for them, listen and interact. Minimise the time you spend on your mobile phone.

ADOLESCENTS: 13–17 YEARS

I want my independence.

I have my own values and don't always agree with my parents.

I have my own friends and can make my own decisions.

I don't always know it, but I need my parents' guidance and benefit from knowing they are there for me.

I understand a lot more and will stop respecting my parents if they constantly fight.

I will stop listening to my parents if I witness them always fighting with each other.

I do not want to be either parent's confidant. I love them both.

I need my parents to provide me with structure and a united front.

- The parenting schedule needs to be flexible.

- Regular scheduled time is still a good thing to do, but also create the possibility for the child to drop in and spend time with you.

- Attend school events.

- Do not confide in your teenager. They will not thank you for the position that puts them in.

- If there are issues, agree a united position before you talk to them. They need the constancy their family provides.

- Do not put your teenager in the middle of your fights. They may be old enough to have opinions but they love you both and will not do well being asked to choose sides.

- Concentrate on your child while you are with them. Be there for them, listen and interact. Minimise the time you spend on your mobile phone.

HELPFUL TIPS

1. Children do not need a perfect parent.

Each day brings fresh challenges for any parent. Do not be too hard on yourself. Your children will come through this.

2. Be aware of your own expectations:

The parenting relationship with your ex-partner should be focused on creating a good working parenting relationship for your children, NOT on either of you fulfilling your own emotional needs. These needs should be met elsewhere in your other close relationships.

3. Create a business partnership:

Many of the best business partnerships are based on a good workplace agreement and not on close friendship. The partners work well together but keep their personal lives separate. This is a good working model for your new parenting relationship. Get into the habit of relating to the other parent in the same way as you would a work colleague.

 - How would you talk to them?
 - How would you approach them with a problem?

Take three deep breaths before speaking, just as you would do in work when you get angry.

4. Use good communication:

What is the best way for you to communicate? It can be very helpful to arrange regular "meetings" with the other parent. This will depend on the age of your children and the amount of things you have to discuss.

a) Arrange a neutral venue.
b) Agree an agenda.
c) Agree not to bring up the past.
d) Set a time limit. Do not discuss difficult issues during the hand-over.

You can also use a notebook to write down everyday information that the other parent needs to know. If texts or e-mails cause rows, do not use that form of communication. Keep conversations short and focused.

5. Separate your couple relationship from your parenting one:

As time goes by, you will each become less important to the other as intimate friends. The parenting relationship is now the future. This can be hard, to say the least, but it is important to now concentrate on seeing your ex-partner as your children's parent.

Try this...

1. List your partner's strengths as a parent.
2. List your partner's shortcomings as a parent.
3. List your strengths as a parent.
4. List your shortcomings as a parent.
5. List your partner's good qualities.
6. List your partner's weaknesses or how you are disappointed in him/her as a mate.
7. List your good qualities as a mate.
8. List how your partner may be disappointed in you.
9. What is important to your spouse about being a parent?
10. What is important to you about being a parent?

(Taken from Lois Gold (1992), Between Love and Hatred, Plume.)

Look at your responses. What are the differences in your parenting styles? Are there ways in which you complement each other?

6. Focus on your child:

The feelings that overwhelm you at the time of separation can blind you to the needs of your child. Take time to think about the hopes and fears your child has. What are their childlike worries? Do they need help to adjust to the new situation? How does your child feel about each of their parents? Asking questions like this can help you to refocus on their needs.

If you consistently criticise the other parent to your child, the child will eventually grow to dislike you for it.

JUST BE PARENTS

Couples who manage to separate their relationship as a couple from their relationship as parents tend to handle their separation or divorce more positively. They put their children's welfare ahead of their own feelings and find a meaningful way forward for their children.

The deep bond that children create between their parents can be temporarily subsumed by the turmoil of a dying relationship. However, underneath everything else lies your continuing love for these little human beings that you created together. This parenting bond ties the parents together and throws them into a new type of life that can feel strange and uncomfortable.

Separating the conflict from the parenting is critical in creating a workable plan for the future. Talking and thinking as the children's parents and not as partners is now the focus.

Children want to freely love both parents without complication. They want to be the subjects of their own lives and not the objects of their parents' squabbles. They cannot take sides or stop loving one of you simply because the other parent requires it of them. They want to be able to attend their own life events, like birthdays and graduations, without worrying about whether their parents can be in the same building together. They never, ever want to have to choose between you.

Children are the future of your family. You may not be married or together anymore, but the best of both of you is in them. As you look ahead, there is a lot to be positive about. You can still be a good parent and you can still raise your children to be happy and secure. It is just a matter of learning to do it in a new way.

Children do come through separation and divorce well, if you make good parenting decisions. Be parents and not estranged lovers.

(5)

AGREEMENT

The agreement that you have both negotiated will be the foundation stone for the next phase of your lives. Where and how you live and how you raise your family will be deeply affected by the nature of the agreement you have drawn up.

It can be easy to lose sight of this, particularly if things are difficult between you. It might feel great to win a row or "get one over on the other" when arguing about things like money or child care. However, there is no doubt that in any agreement you will each need the other to deal fairly with you. Just as your ex-partner is looking for compromise from you on one issue, you will be looking for the same from them on another.

PREPARING A FULL AGREEMENT

If your **solicitor** has already been representing you on all aspects of your separation, you will already have a good idea of what the full separation will involve.

If you have been negotiating through **mediation**, your mediator will be drawing up a document at the end of the process outlining all that has been agreed between you and your ex-partner. If you wish, you will then be able to go to a solicitor to legalise this document.

If you and your ex-partner have **negotiated your own** agreement, it is important to consider having the complete agreement drawn up and legalised in the appropriate way.

Regardless of which road you have gone down, it can be helpful to get an overview of what a final agreement will include. The following is an outline of the main issues you would be covering and the information needed.

General/preamble

Main issues to discuss:
Are you both in agreement to formally separate?

If no, you may need to consider a contested separation or divorce and will need to take good legal advice on how to proceed.
If yes, you are about to proceed with an uncontested separation or divorce.

Information you will need:

- Proof of marriage.
- Names of children.
- Date of marriage.
- Dates of birth of children.
- Place of marriage.
- If you have already separated, date of separation.

Written clauses may look like this...

1. We take full responsibility for this agreement and undertake to live by its terms in good faith.

   (where you plan to legalise the mediated agreement)

2. We agree that we will legalise this mediated agreement and will undertake to do so through our solicitors.

   OR

   We agree that this agreement will be incorporated into our divorce.

3. We married each other on 15/04/1992 in St Andrew's Church, Dublin.

4. We have been living separately since 2/10/2010.

   OR

   We agreed to live separately from each other from 30/09/2011.

5. Our children's names are: Betty, Anne and John. Their dates of birth are as follows: Betty: 05/03/1994, Anne: 07/06/1997, John: 15/07/2001.

6. We respect the need for each of us to build new and separate lives. We will also respect each other's right to privacy.

7. We agree that we will pay for the cost of legalising our agreement in the following way: We will share the costs of legalising this document between us and will be responsible for our own legal costs separate from this agreement.

Children

Main issues to discuss

1.   Are you clear how decisions concerning the children are going to be made?
2.   Have you a clear parenting schedule that everyone knows and understands?
3.   Have you and your partner agreed how to discuss the potential for flexibility in the schedule or matters as they arise?

Information you will need:

Everything should be within the parenting plan.

The parenting plan may look like this:

1.   As joint guardians of [names of children], we agree that all major decisions affecting the health, education and welfare of [names of children] will be made jointly between us. On a day-to-day basis, we intend sharing our parenting responsibilities as set out below:

2.   Parenting plan:

	Monday	Tuesday	Wednesday	Thursday	Friday	Saturday	Sunday
Week 1	M	D	D	M	M	D	M
Week 2	M	M	M	D	M	D	D
Week 3	M	D	D	M	M	D	M
Week 4	M	M	M	D	M	D	D

Mum = *M*

Dad = *D*

Summer Holidays, etc.

School Holidays
What child-care arrangements do you need to put in place for school holidays?

We agree that we will organise child care for our children as follows:

School summer holidays: (timetable)
Mid-term breaks: (timetable)
Bank holidays: (timetable)
Christmas break: (timetable)
In-service days: (timetable)

How will you share the school holiday child-care responsibilities?
We agree to share the responsibility for the child care as follows: (timetable)

What about Bank Holidays?
We agree to share the responsibility for the child care as follows: (timetable)

Holidays with Children
What arrangements would you like to make for going on holiday with the children?
When does each of you need to notify work of your planned leave?
Therefore, at what point in the year do you need to have decided on holiday dates?

Christmas and New Year
A clear plan for this holiday should be negotiated well in advance. Sometimes parents agree:
- To alternate Christmas Day with each other.
- To share the day.
- To have this day as the one day they do spend time with the children together.

Child Care and Babysitting
Each of you will need a babysitter from time to time. Do you:

- Phone the other first, remembering that the other is entitled to say no on their night off?
- Agree a shortlist of babysitters you are both happy with that you can use?

Birthdays and Other Special Days

Children will remember if you have rowed over their birthday. Sometimes parents agree the following:

> - We agree to discuss and agree plans for _____ a month before, in order to give our child the best possible birthday.

Education/School Meetings

1. We are both satisfied with the present arrangements for the children's education and we agree to review these arrangements as required (or as they reach primary, secondary or third level).

2. We agree to keep each other fully informed of educational progress of [names of children] by exchanging copies of their report(s) and by attending parent/teacher meetings, either together or separately, as appropriate.

Communication

1. We agree that, while our children are spending time with either one of us, they may contact the other parent.

2. We agree that the absent parent may contact the children by phone/skype or other alternative form of communication at a reasonable time.

Passports and Travel

1. We understand that in order for our children to obtain passports in their own right, we need to give our consent as their parents (joint guardians). We therefore agree to give whatever consent is necessary when required. _____ will take care of the passports.

2. a) We both consent to the other parent taking [names of children] out of the State for holiday purposes only.

OR

b) We agree that we will obtain each other's consent to take our children out of the State for holiday purposes only; this consent should not be unreasonably withheld.

FINANCE

Main issues to discuss:

An agreement on how the children's costs will be met is the most important part of this section.

There may also be spousal support, which is often taxed differently from child support. It is important to contact Inland Revenue to establish what is the best course for your future taxation.

Does there need to be an insurance policy to guarantee that child and/or spousal support can still be paid in the event of a change of circumstances?

What agreement is there in place to pay for the family's medical health insurance? Who will be responsible for the payments?

How will dental and optical procedures be paid for?

Have you made a list of your assets and decided how to divide them?

Have you made a list of your debts and decided who will be responsible for which debt?

If your debts are to be paid off as part of the sale of the family home or other asset, have you an agreed list of which debts will be paid off? Have you agreed when this transaction will take place?

Information you will need:

1.   You will be asked to provide full financial information with documentation (see Chapter 2 on finance).

2.   Make sure you have included everything. Do not leave anything out as this can cause tension and difficulty later on.

3.   Details of your tax status, pension(s), and life insurance and assurance.

4   A list of all assets with current value.

5.   A list of all debt with current value.

Written clauses may look like this...

1. Jim is employed by OGX Stationers, Baggot St, as an accounts manager. He earns €55,000 gross per annum, giving him a net income of €4,500 per month.

2. Mary is self-employed as a part-time physiotherapist. Her gross annual income is €26,000, giving her a net monthly income of €2,300 per month.

3. Mary receives Child Benefit of €250 from the Department of Social Protection.

4. Having looked at our financial needs and the needs of our children, we have agreed that Jim will pay as financial support to Mary and our children the sum of €1,200 for each month, divided as follows:

   €300 to Mary
   €300 for each child

The total payment will be made by standing order on the first working day of each month into Mary's Bank account (no. _____).

Review of Financial Arrangements

We agree that we will review this financial agreement if either of our financial or domestic circumstances change.

Income Tax

1. We are separately assessed for tax purposes and agree to carry on being assessed in this way.

OR

2. We are jointly assessed for tax purposes and agree to carry on being assessed in this way.

OR

3. We are jointly assessed for tax purposes and have agreed to change to separate assessment. We agree to notify the Revenue Commissioners to this effect.

Assets and Debts

1. We have the following assets:

   1(a)   We have agreed the following:

2. We have the following debts:

   2(a)   We have agreed the following:

We agree that each of us will be responsible for any personal debts incurred by us from the date of this mediated agreement and will not hold the other person liable.

Medical/dental/optical

Main issues to discuss:

- What agreement is there in place to pay for the family's medical health insurance?
- How will you pay for the family's medical bills?
- Who will be responsible for the payments?
- How will dental work be paid for?

Information you will need:

Details of health insurance policies.

Written clauses may look like this...

1. We have agreed to share equally the costs of any dental or optical treatment. We agree to discuss how we will do this before any treatment starts.

2. Jim has agreed to pay for medical insurance for himself and the three children. Mary agrees to pay for her own. Jim will provide Mary with the details of the children's policy.

Family home

Main issues to discuss:

- Do you have a plan that can be implemented?
- If a buy-out or re-mortgage is needed, has a lending institution made a viable offer?
- Are the payments manageable?
- Will you need to pay capital gains tax?

Information you will need:

- Valuation of the family home.
- Details of: The present mortgage and new mortgage (if required).
                  Mortgage protection.
                  Contents insurance.

Written clauses may look like this...

The family home at 155 Sunflower Drive, Clontarf, Dublin is held in our joint names. We value this property at €500,000 and there is an outstanding mortgage of €150,000 with ERK Building Society.

We agree that Mary will continue to live in the family home until the children reach the ages of either 18 or 23. At this time we will discuss and agree on what to do with the family home.

OR

We have decided to sell the family home. We have agreed to put it on the market with a reserve of €500,000. We have agreed to pay the outstanding mortgage from the equity before splitting the rest 60% to Mary and 40% to Jim.

OR

Jim agrees to transfer his entire interest in the family home to Mary. Mary will pay Jim the sum of €80,000. Mary shall be liable for mortgage repayments and shall indemnify Jim against any liability in respect of these payments from the time of the property transfer.

Contents of the family home

Main issues to discuss:

There are many aspects to dividing the contents of the home. Some things have sentimental value and there is also the practicality of how to furnish a second home. It can be helpful to make a list and agree a time to work your way through the list.

Sometimes couples agree that whoever has to pay for new essentials, such as beds, linen, kitchen appliances, etc, will have some money, commensurate with the cost, from the assets to do so.

Information you will need:

- A list of contents that need to be discussed and split between you.
- A list of goods that need to be bought for the second home.

Written clauses may look like this...

1. Jim has agreed to take his personal belongings and the list of items already agreed between us. The rest of the household contents will remain in the family home.

OR

2. We have already agreed on how to divide the contents of the family home.

OR

3. Please see the attached list of items divided, as agreed, between us.

Life policies

Main issues to discuss:

Do you want to retain or cancel these policies?

Information you will need:

Details of any life policies either of you may have.

Written clauses may look like this...

1. We intend to cancel our existing insurance policies.

OR

2. Jim agrees to pay the premiums on the following life insurance policies:

3. Mary agrees to pay the premiums on the following life insurance policies:

Pensions

Main issues to discuss:

Pensions can amount to a considerable sum of money. There are specific rules and laws for pensions and any agreement you make will have to fit within those.

- Do you know how much your pensions are worth?
- Have you decided what to do?
- Is this possible under the terms of the pension plan?

Information you will need:

Details of any pension you have.

Written clauses may look like this...

1. Mary agrees that she shall not be regarded as the spouse or dependant of Jim for any of the purposes of the pension scheme of which he is a member. She renounces any rights she may have in any such pension scheme and directs the trustees/administration to disregard her for the purposes of the pension scheme. We agree to instruct our solicitors to carry out any necessary legal proceedings.

OR

2. Jim agrees that he shall continue to regard Mary as his spouse for the purposes of his pension scheme. Jim agrees that he will not interfere with any rights to which Mary is now or may become entitled to, arising out of any such pension scheme. We agree to instruct our solicitors to carry out any necessary legal proceedings.

OR

3. We agree that all matters concerning the pension entitlements of either of us will be dealt with during the course of divorce proceedings.

INHERITANCE RIGHTS AND WILLS

Succession is the term used to describe the inheritance of a person's property on their death. This property might include the family home, money in the bank, stocks and shares, other houses or land, business interests and their belongings.

Each country has a set of laws to help decide how succession should be handled. These laws may give the surviving partner automatic rights to a share in the estate of the deceased person. These are called succession rights. This is particularly the case if you are or have been married or in a civil partnership.

Even if you have made a will, your surviving partner could be legally entitled to an appropriate share regardless. The fact that you may have lived separately for many years does not necessarily affect these entitlements. It is only when you divorce that succession rights are automatically extinguished.

If you simply live apart or opt for a legal separation, you can choose to renounce these succession rights. Before doing this, it is worthwhile taking good legal advice.

A divorced spouse or a civil partner whose civil partnership has been dissolved can apply to the court to seek a share of the estate of their former spouse/civil partner.

WILLS

A will is a document which is witnessed by two witnesses. It sets out in writing what you would like to happen to your possessions (called your estate) in the event of your death.

It is important for you to make a will because, if you do not, the law will decide what happens to your property. A will can ensure that good arrangements are made for your dependants and that your property is distributed in the way you would like after you die.

Good questions to ask...

1. Who will look after the children?
2. What provisions do I need to make for our children?
3. Who do I trust to make sure the terms of my will are carried through?
4. Do I need to consult my partner about any aspect of my will?
5. Do I have all the information I need to make good decisions about this?

LOOKING AHEAD TO THE FUTURE

When you have your agreement drawn up and in your hand it is time to look to the future. Did everything go your way in the separation/divorce? Probably not, but isn't that life? Whatever you have "won or lost" it is what you make of the agreement you have that will determine its success in your life.

Try this...

Before you sign, ask yourself:

- Can I live with this agreement?
- Is this fair enough for both of us and our family?
- Can we parent our children the way we want to with this agreement?
- Can I accept the things I don't like in this agreement, in order to move on?
- How will I feel about this in five years' time?

After you sign:

- How do I move on?
- How do I make the most of my life?

It may be that your future is not quite as you imagined it would be. You may not have wanted your marriage to end, or have had to agree to something in the separation agreement that you really find difficult. No doubt there will be imperfections in your separation plan, and you may have regrets, but the choice of how you live your life is in your hands.

ACCEPTANCE

The loss of a loving relationship can give pain beyond the imaginable. It can deny us the ability to feel "rational" and take away our ability to think clearly. Negotiating a long and complex divorce or separation settlement on top of such feelings can be unbearable at times.

However, a point does come when the regrets of the past become eclipsed by hope for the future and we learn to live with a new type of daily routine. It can take a long time to reach this point and some days may be more difficult than others, but time passes and things do improve.

It becomes time to accept the things that we cannot change and move on.

Try this...

1. After you have signed your separation or divorce agreement, do something positive to mark your changed life. You may not feel like doing anything too upbeat, but try to think of something that would help you to feel more optimistic about the future.

2. If you are very busy, try and take some time to reflect on what has happened. Don't avoid the feelings you have at this time.

3. When you feel yourself getting down, phone a close friend or plan something positive.

4. Make a list of things you would like to do in life that you have not yet managed to do, and see how many you can achieve.

If you feel that you are really struggling, seek help through your GP or phone a counsellor.

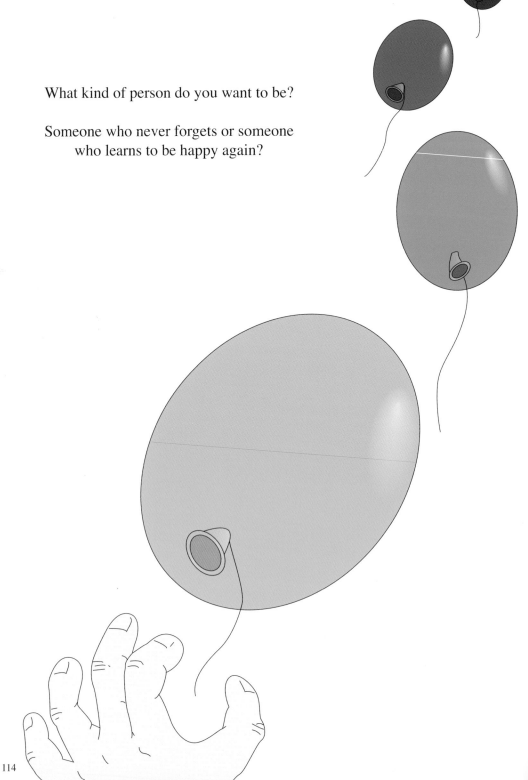

What kind of person do you want to be?

Someone who never forgets or someone
who learns to be happy again?

FORGIVENESS

> *"In forgiveness there is a recognition that nothing we do to punish the other person will heal us.... A choice to forgive is a choice to heal yourself."*
>
> – Lois Gold

Forgiveness can only be given freely. With the ability to forgive comes the feeling of freedom and hope for the future. We take away the other person's power and transform our own lives for the better.

Forgiveness is a process of letting go and looking to the future. We start to take back our sense of self and stop living through our reaction to someone else. Forgiveness is not about agreeing with the other person that what happened was okay. It is about releasing ourselves from the continuing hurt and suffering that the experience has created in us.

The starting point for forgiving is to want to do so and to realise that it may take a long time. Forgiveness comes from understanding how you have been hurt and angered by what has happened, and then finding a way to let go.

Here are some questions that might help:

- What does forgiveness mean for you?
- What is it that you find hard to forgive?
- What would your life be like if you could forgive the other person?
- What feelings do you have at this time?
- What would it be like if you did not have these feelings?
- Could you separate the person from their actions?
- How would you have liked the other person to have acted instead?
- What do you recognise as good in the other person?
- What do you think they may say about you?
- Could there be anything you did that they could find difficult to forgive?
- What would both your lives be like if you could both forgive?

Forgiveness is a process of letting go of the past. It is our choice and within our control.

115

MAKING IT WORK

Your separation will not be perfect. You may have to accept some things you do not like and make decisions about problems that were not of your making. However, at this point you are at the end of one part of your life and at the start of a new part.

It is not the decisions demanded by the agreement that are inherently good or bad but what you make of the decisions that counts. You have to make a good life for yourself and it is in your hands to make it work.

It will not always be easy... but then life is rarely so. Some days will be harder than others, but your new life will slowly settle into its own patterns.

If you are parenting with your ex-partner, remember:

1. If arguments happen, try not to talk about them in front of the children.
2. Make the hand-overs as easy as possible for the children.
3. Arrange to meet to discuss issues in advance of any situation arising.
4. Plan family celebrations well so you do not have any misunderstandings.
5. Let go of the past. Do not allow resentment to build up, leading to arguments.

Time will make a difference in how you feel about your separation. As the months and years pass, the hurt and experiences of this time will begin to fade.

(6)

EXPERIENCES

The following short stories are based on conversations with real people about real feelings and experiences. We have changed the names of those involved and certain details to protect identities. Some of the stories show both sides of the same story.

Lost Dreams
The experiences of a husband and wife
Staying Put
Different views of a husband and wife
The Rows Never Stop
The regrets of a couple
Telling the Family – The Children
A father's story
Telling the Family – The Parents
A woman and her mother
Telling the Siblings
When it goes wrong
New Partners
Ex-wife's new relationship
Getting Over the Guilt
A husband reflects
Feeling Independent
A woman finds her feet, two years on
Legal Battling
Managing to communicate, eighteen months on
Money, Money, Money
How mediation can help sort out money
After the mediation session
Moving On
A number of stories about moving on
Moving On – The Children
A number of stories about moving on from the children's perspective
What Kids Say
Children's feelings about separation

LOST DREAMS
A wife's experience

So, this woman with a little boy in a buggy came up to me in the street. "He's your husband's." she said. I stared at her. She said it again, "He's your husbands and he is three years old." I still couldn't believe what I was hearing. I looked at the little boy in the buggy... he looked like my daughter. This was her half brother.... My world came crashing in.

That was six months ago. My husband moved out. He is living in a flat. I don't know if he is seeing her or not but I don't care anymore. My life is in tatters. He gives us money, me and the girls, but I can hardly face him when he comes to the door.

I smile and stay calm... for my girls... they still love him so I have to be strong. How can I hate him, love him, not care about him and stay calm all at the same time? Those moments on the doorstep waving my girls...our girls...off. It breaks my heart. They love him but he left them. I know he says he just left me but, to them, he is gone.

I know that I will start to get over this sometime. This feeling of anger and betrayal... but what about the shattering of my dreams? We were a family, we were going to grow old together. We loved each other.... We had just moved house for goodness sake!

All the time he had another child. How do you account for that? This man I thought I knew, taking my future away so casually.

When I think of the future I dare to hope. I dare to hope that I will find someone and I will be happy again. For the moment, I love my girls and they love their mum and dad. So, I need to stay calm, smile and carry on....

LOST DREAMS
A husband's experience

Here I am with four children and I don't live with any of them! I'm not sure how it happened. One minute I was part of a family and was enjoying an affair. I know it was wrong but it just happened like that. Then my little man was born and I was so happy. I had my three beautiful girls and now a son.

It was all a bit mad, keeping it a secret from my wife, but these things happen. I know I hurt her tremendously. I hate thinking about that. She looks so sad... and I did that to her. Well, maybe we were not that happy anyway. That's probably why I had the affair.

I do love my children. They are so clever and great fun. I see my girls at the weekend and I pop in during the week to say hello. It is hard to go back to my home like that but I try and keep calm and happy for the girls. They love their mum and I want them to. She is there for them every day. I can't be anymore.

The bit that hurts the most is the fact that they think I left them too. I have tried to explain but they are too young to understand. Their faces on the day I moved out were something I will never forget.

If could turn back time, what would I do? I don't know. If I hadn't met my son's mother I wouldn't have my boy..... But the pain I have caused my family is hard to think about.

I know that I am a good dad and that is what I can do well. I will be there for my kids and I'll try and work the rest out as I go.

STAYING PUT
A husband's view

It was my wife who decided that we should separate. She said that she was not able to live in this dead marriage anymore. She had given us long enough and it was over. Dead marriage? I was surprised... shocked. I know things weren't great but we got on okay. There were no real arguments, no big bust ups. She says we fell out of love. I thought that we still cared enough about each other to make it work.

The thing that really makes me angry is that she says it is over and I have to move out.... Apparently it is me who loses my home, me who sleeps in a grotty flat and me who stops living with my children.

Since when did her well-being become more important than me being a dad?

I will not move out under any circumstances! We have three beautiful kids and I am going to be here for them. I don't want to be a weekend father or a McDonald's dad. I am their dad, that means 24/7: for homework, bedtimes and breakfasts... nothing less.

Why does the man always do the moving out? I could live with her quite happily. I like my home. I love my kids. I care about her. All she loses is a husband she doesn't want but I lose everything. No way! I have worked too hard for all of this. I will fight this. She can't make me do it and the kids need me here.

STAYING PUT
A wife's view

I don't know how much more I can take of this. We live in the same house but can't sit in the same room as each other. We love the same children but can't agree on how to be their parents. We share the same marriage but have nothing to say to each other.

Can he not see what it is doing to us? What it is doing to the kids and me? He is so stubborn. It is all about him and his needs. Well, he has to go. He just has to. What does he think we can do?

I am the one who looks after the kids. I am home every day after work to do homework and feed them. He is never home until 8.00 p.m. He is out in the morning. Don't get me wrong, he has always worked hard. He provides for us well. But he and I have nothing in common.

All this business about being a dad. The kids know he's their dad. I won't stop him seeing them. They love him. In fact, things will be better when he moves out. He has to be the one that moves. I can't afford to. I only work part time and if I am not here for the kids then who will be? Is he going to get a child minder?

It makes no sense. Deep down he knows the marriage is over. We both do. I am so sorry and sad about it all, but I can't make it better anymore.

THE ROWS NEVER STOP
The regrets of a couple

We have been separated for three years and we still can't be in the same room. We just make each other so angry.

We met twelve years ago. We got on like a house on fire and fell in love. When we got married we were so happy. We adored each other and had such fun. Our two kids were born, a boy and a girl, and our family was complete. It is hard to know how things started to change.

There were little niggles, small fights. We hurt each other. Things got worse. Our home stopped being a calm place... it felt tense all the time. The children stayed outside playing with their friends or went to their room. They knew the signs. First there would be the icy silence, then the sharp word. The air would change as we traded insults. We would scream and shout, not caring who heard. I can feel it now, the anger, the hurt. I feel sick thinking about some of the things he said to me.

Our friends didn't really know what was going on but they stopped calling round. He went out with his friends and I went out with mine. They were great. I used to talk about him all the time. My friends said I should stick up for myself. His friends said the same to him. There was one friend who tried to stop us.

I remember what he said. He asked us if we were going to keep on like this. Point scoring and judging each other. He said that we were about to lose ourselves to this fight. We didn't listen.

We even argued in mediation. We were trying to sort out our money. He didn't seem to get the fact that I didn't have enough to support the girls. He kept saying over and over I should work more hours, take in a lodger or cut down our spending. I used to shout back at him that he didn't care about his family. The mediator talked to us about how we sparked each other. The anger that we felt was so strong it clouded out everything else.

I remember what she said. She asked us something. She asked us if we thought our fighting might be a way of avoiding the sadness of our parting. If we kept fighting, we would not have to face the reality of being alone... apart.

We ignored the question, left mediation and headed for court. Our fight was made for court. We fought every step of the way. Our solicitors gave us what we needed: the feeling that each of us was right. We each felt justified in holding our ground.

I do remember one thing my solicitor said, though. He asked me if all this fighting was costing me my family life. He talked about how we should remember that this would all be over one day and we would still be parents of the same children.

We didn't listen and sat in the courtroom glaring at each other. The judge took the responsibility of making the decisions from us. We could blame him, if we didn't get what we wanted. The judge asked us if we loved our children. We said yes. Then he said that he didn't love them, in fact he had never met them, and yet we wanted him to decide about their future. He wondered why we couldn't do this ourselves, despite professing our parental love for them.

We ignored him and carried on.

I look back and wonder about all of this. Did we have times when we could have stopped?

The people who could see what was happening had tried to make us see that we could have chosen how we split up. We could have remembered what we used to appreciate in each other and remember to be parents.

We found it too easy to blame each other and not own up to our part in the fight. When you get that angry you pretend that you want it all to stop when, in fact, you want the other to change and yourself to win. What a waste of time, what a waste of money and what a waste of a family.

When we left the court on the final day of our divorce hearing, I thought I would be so happy. But I was just exhausted. And the funny thing was that the next day he was coming to pick up the children. We had torn each other apart and now we had to get on with our lives, still parenting our children.

And it's not like the written agreement we got was much different. It was almost the same as what we would have reached in mediation and what our solicitors were prepared to settle on. We could have saved a lot of time and money, but we had to have our fight.

I see him sitting in the car, building up the courage to knock on the door. He hates coming to the home he once lived in. The kids look at me nervously. They think there are going to be more hot words, more tension. I look out. The kids have their school play this Friday. They are more worried about how we will behave than whether they remember their lines or not.

So, here we are. Him sitting in the car and me waiting at the door with the kids. Maybe time will help. If I knew then what the fighting would do to us, how long it would go on for and how much hurt it would cause, I would have done things differently.

TELLING THE FAMILY – THE CHILDREN
A father's story

I don't think either of us will ever forget telling our three children we were separating. My wife and I talked for months about how to tell them. We had decided to separate after years of trying to make it work. It was just over and we both knew it. We had no idea if our kids had guessed anything was wrong. Our middle girl had asked a few things but we didn't know what to say to her.

We had decided to tell them together. The books said that this was best and we were determined to get this right. However, the thought of it was almost too much to bear.

We sat them down one evening after dinner. We had agreed that my wife would start, but as she opened her mouth the tears started to fall. My daughter looked at her. "You're splitting up, aren't you?" she said. There was silence. The children looked at us. We looked at each other and then at them. "Yes, we are," I said.

I was amazed that they knew so much. The little one was shocked but the other two said that they had been expecting this for some time. We told them we loved them and that we were still their mum and dad and nothing would change that. They asked us where they would live. We said we were not sure but we hoped to keep the family home for them.

My son was angry. He was angry that we had not told him sooner. He had been worrying. He has a friend whose parents fight all the time. They had just lost their house. We tried to assure him that this would not happen to us.

Our youngest asked, "If you're not fighting any more why don't you stay together?" That was a tricky one to answer. My wife told her that we just couldn't live together and that, now we had decided not to, it had helped us to stop fighting. I don't think the little one understood but that's all we could say.

Over the weeks the kids asked us lots of questions. Some we could answer but others we couldn't. We were as honest as we could be. They were angry at us, upset that their lives were changing and worried a lot of the time.

Part of our plan at that time was to take the kids out now and again, one at a time, so we could talk. I took my lad out bowling and to the football. My wife took our daughter into town and the little one had trips to the seaside and park. Sometimes we talked about the future, but a lot of the time we talked about other things.

My wife and I hurt each other a lot over the years. There were days when we couldn't look at each other, but somehow we managed to work together as parents. Telling the kids was hard. Being there for them was awkward when they asked those difficult questions but they came through the separation alright.

Our children still have their family. It is a separated family, but they have us and each other.

We don't have all the answers for them but when they look back at that time I think they can say, "When mum and dad split up they did the best they could to be good parents... and they were."

TELLING THE FAMILY – THE PARENTS
A woman and her mother

My parents were very upset when we separated. They said to me that we should stay together for the kids, that marriage was for life and we were giving up too easily. I kept saying to them that they didn't understand. They didn't know what was going on.

After that they never phoned the house. They stopped talking to my husband and were strange with me. I eventually had enough. I went round to the house one Sunday and asked them what was going on. My dad said nothing but Mum was upset. She said that they didn't know what to do. The day I had arrived to their house and blurted out the news she had been shocked. She liked my husband and didn't want to lose him as a son-in-law. She thought that it might pass and we would change our minds.

She said she just wanted me to be happy. I remember her looking at me and asking "What about the kids? We love them. They're our grandchildren." I said to her that they would always be their grandchildren and they missed her. Then we cried and talked for a long time.

My husband and I went to mediation. We told our parents that we were negotiating a plan and when we were organised we would tell them what we were going to do. We asked them to be there for the kids. To take them out and give them some fun while we tried to work out our lives. We also asked them to support us both, if they could.

It was hard, really hard, but we got there. When we had our agreement sorted we arranged to go together to my parents and then his. We sat down and told them that the house would be sold and we were going to have two separate places. We said it was time to put the past behind us and try to start new lives. We thanked them for supporting our family and asked them to do three things:

1. To love and support the children, and not to say anything bad about either of us to them.
2. To respect that this had been hard on us both and that we needed help from our mums and dads to move on.
3. To keep in touch with the other person, if they wished.

They liked the fact that we asked for help and the three things gave them something they knew they could do.

I meet my own in-laws now and again. At first it was a bit strained. Now we can chat away about the kids and the weather. It was worth thinking about them. It helped having them on both our sides.

TELLING THE SIBLINGS
When it goes wrong

When I told my sister she said, "Well, anyone who wants to leave you is mad! He is quite clearly out of his mind." She phoned my brother immediately and told him he couldn't play golf with my husband anymore because he was a scumbag.

So that was that, the battle lines were drawn, whether I liked it or not, and war was declared. I actually quite liked it, to be honest. I could go round to my sister's and give out about my husband as much as I wanted and she was ready to believe everything I said. My brother had been friends with my husband for years. In fact, that is how we met. Now he wouldn't give him the time of day. It is funny how others feel they have to take sides on your behalf.

It all got out of hand when my brother told my husband that he had to find another pub to drink in. "Nobody wants to drink with a cheater," he shouted. There was a bit of a scuffle. Nobody was hurt but it was bad enough. I was glad. I was glad that my brother had stood up for me. I wanted my husband to feel bad about what he had done. It was what he deserved.

It carried on like this until my daughter's birthday. We were having lunch at the house when the row happened. My sister told my husband what she thought of him. He told her she was an interfering old b****. Neither knew that our daughter was listening. My daughter ran out the house crying and was missing for three hours. I was frantic. My husband was worried sick. That was when I grew up.

I realised that getting my family to fight for me, like we were still kids, was not the way to live. My children were in the middle. I was stressed out. The fight was getting bigger and bigger and soon it would engulf us all.

I sat down with my brother and sister. I reminded my brother that he had been friends with my husband since childhood and maybe things had to change, but not like this. I thanked them for caring enough about me to stick up for me, but now I was ready to build bridges for the sake of my kids and the family. I told them I needed their support.

It took a long time to sort things out. My ex-husband and I are now divorced and can talk to each other alright. The golf games are back on. I don't think it is quite the same, but they get along. My sister takes my kids out with her two and has agreed with them not to talk about the divorce. She spoils them, as all good aunties should, and they enjoy themselves.

My ex-husband's family were never as angry as my own. I see them from time to time and they come to the kids' birthdays. I do it for the children and, as time has gone on, it has got easier. To start with we didn't know what to say to each other so we stuck to safe subjects. Now we are more relaxed. Life moves on.

NEW PARTNERS

Ex-wife's new relationship

My ex-wife and I got divorced three years ago. She is living in the family home with our two kids and I have a house quite nearby. She bought me out of the family home and so I bought this one. It all worked out fine and I have the kids to stay regularly.

I had said that I never wanted anyone else to stay in the family home with my kids. My wife had laughed and told me that there was no way she would ever want a relationship again. I suppose time changes a lot of things.

I heard about John from the kids. They had gone to the zoo with their mum and her friend. That was fine, but, after hearing about John a few times, I noticed that the kids stopped talking about him. "That's good," I thought. "He has obviously not lasted long." I was wrong.

The children were a bit awkward when I asked them about their mum. They didn't like to talk about their other home anymore. I couldn't decide what was wrong... and then I got the phone call. It was my ex-wife. She wanted to meet up to discuss something with me.

My ex told me she had met someone, John, and that it was serious. She wanted to introduce him to me before she told the children that he was her new partner. I told her that I thought they had already guessed and that she should have told me sooner. I was hurt and angry... and I wasn't sure why. We both knew this would happen to one of us sooner or later. Maybe I was annoyed it wasn't me!

I met John and actually quite liked him. He said he cared about the kids but wouldn't get in my way as their dad. I told him that he was damn right... he wouldn't. We laughed and it was very awkward. The kids got on with him and they were a lot more relaxed once they knew I was okay with it. I made sure I seemed okay, but it took a lot of getting used to.

Six months later, John moved into my old family home. I remember the day as if it was yesterday. I felt sick with bitterness. Another man with his feet under my table. Living in the house I fixed up. Sitting at the breakfast table and getting my kids out to school. My ex did talk to me about it. We agreed new parenting rules and John sticks to them. I don't want him punishing my kids or giving out to them... that's my job. We had a few rows and in the end we just agreed to try and get along for the sake of the kids.

It will be a while before I feel alright about this. Don't get me wrong, getting a divorce was the right thing and I want my ex to be happy. I just don't want to feel as if I have lost everything else.

GETTING OVER THE GUILT
A husband reflects

The first five months of the separation were just awful. I felt so guilty about how the whole thing had happened. It really got to me and brought me down. My wife and I didn't want to hurt each other, but we did. Our children were stuck in the middle and then I left.

No matter how I felt, I had to go to work every day. I have my own business and I had to get up in the morning and function. My mind was a confused mess. I would stare at things for hours. Work reports that normally would take me half an hour stayed on my desk unfinished. Colleagues who relied on me had to fend for themselves.

I would start to eat and then stop, walk into my office and then back out again... and all the time I had this dreadful feeling of guilt over the separation. I don't even know how the feeling started, but I really felt to blame.

Eventually my accountant of all people asked to meet me. He gave it to me straight. The business was beginning to suffer and he was worried about me. He told me that he had a brother who had gone through a split and he recognised the signs. He suggested I go to my GP. Actually he *told* me to go to my GP. I did and she referred me to a counsellor.

Things began to get better. I did a lot of talking, not something I had done before, and slowly the guilt began to lift. I started eating, work became an interesting challenge again and life began to make sense to me. I started to rebuild my world day by day.

I underestimated what I would feel when my wife and I separated. I thought I would be okay. I think there is a difference between feeling guilty but not letting it get to you and becoming totally consumed by the feeling. I nearly went under.

It is natural to have all sorts of feelings at a time like separation. It is a crisis and it would be strange if you didn't struggle. I know that now. I would tell anyone like me to ask for help. It makes a difference and you will start to recover.

FEELING INDEPENDENT
A woman finds her feet, two years on…

When my marriage finished, I felt lost. My husband packed up and left and there I was on my own. We had been together for 15 years and a lot of those had been good. I collapsed in an emotional heap. I didn't know how to be single!

My solicitor suggested that I work towards a complete feeling of independence. He said it would help me if I handled my own affairs, so I sorted out my own accounts, electricity, health insurance. It was a bit daunting at first but I began to enjoy managing my own life.

I could have relied on my solicitor to sort out the separation but he told me that this would not help me in the long run. He insisted that I keep my own notes and make my own decisions. He was right. I followed his advice and it has worked.

We finally agreed on our divorce this month and I felt confident about going into court. We have a good agreement and I think we managed to be fair to each other. I didn't get everything I wanted but, then, neither did my husband, so I suppose that counts as fair.

Anyway, I walked out of court knowing that I was okay on my own. I could take charge of my life and had all my bills, money and accounts in order. I liked that.

LEGAL BATTLING
Managing to communicate, eighteen months on…

The solicitors got involved and we were told not to talk to each other. There was a lot of mistrust and it just got worse and worse. We were both afraid that whatever we said would be used against us. We had no communication at all in the end.

I couldn't believe that it had come to this. We had been married for twelve years, had three children and a business together and now we couldn't even ask one another to pass the milk without a courtroom drama. Every time I talked to my solicitors they told me to stay strong and not to give in. I had to be careful not to be taken in by false promises from the other side. I am sure he was being told the same. It was all so tough and hard nosed. We had no idea how to act around each other when we were with the kids.

For the whole duration of the divorce proceedings, life was unbearable. He accused me of ripping him off; I accused him of deserting his children. We were so bitter. The anger would consume us as we fought it all out. And all the time we couldn't talk, really talk, like we used to.

Then the battle was over, the papers were signed and all was settled. Almost immediately, things calmed down. We still had the hurt but the battle was gone. Things are becoming increasingly calmer and we are actually almost friends again.

MONEY, MONEY, MONEY

How mediation can help sort out money

Mary

We started going to mediation to work out all our finances. I couldn't manage on the money he was giving me and I knew he needed to give me more. We have three kids and a mortgage. I work part time so my income goes back out, almost as soon as it comes in.

Jim

I don't know where Mary thinks I am going to get this extra money from. My wages are the same as when we lived under the one roof, and we didn't have enough then. This mediation is going to have to show her that you can't get blood out of a stone.

Mary

I sat down and filled in my budget sheet. My God, I can't believe what we spend on the children. The bills are no better. I know we have a summer holiday and try and get away for a few days in the winter, but we need the break. At least John will see that I am not blowing his money!

Jim

My solicitor says that I don't have to pay Mary what she is asking. He says she will have to cope with what she gets. I need to pay for somewhere to live and have a life as well. This budget sheet shows how much I need. Wait until she sees the real cost of living apart.

After the mediation session

Mary

Well, that was not what I was expecting. When the mediator added all our numbers together and we saw the joint cost of everything, I got a shock. I had never thought of it like that. The two houses and the children's costs coming out of the one pot of money. I know Jim and I earn quite well, but when you see it added together and then put it beside our joint expenses it doesn't look nearly enough.

Jim

That was the first time I saw all of the costs written down like that. I can see that we need to tighten our belts, but if I give less to Mary for the kids they will have to stop their sports, and I don't want that. I never thought of sorting out the money this way.

If Mary and I can sit down and agree on some mutual savings maybe we can look at the maintenance differently. Whether we like it or not, we are still in this together.

MOVING ON

Jane, 47

"I never thought I would get through this, but I have. It's about 18 months after my husband and I parted, and I have started to feel my personality change. I feel more positive and full of energy. I have started to think of new things I could do and life doesn't seem so full of worry and confusion.

I think the most important thing for me was the fact that I had friends and that I could talk to them. I sort of talked myself out of my depression and loneliness... and you do feel alone when you separate. I quite like that feeling now. My independence is something I am proud of. For a long time I was part of a couple and then, when that stopped, I felt as if my right arm had been taken off. I had to start all over again... but I did!"

Alan, 65

"My divorce was ten years ago. I have a new partner, my kids are grown up and life goes on. I look back and almost can't remember what we fought about. We couldn't agree on anything and we ended up in court. It was expensive and painful, but it was all so long ago now.

Our daughter got married last year. What a great day that was! We were so proud of her and she looked beautiful. My ex-wife actually hugged me and said that we had at least got one thing right. Our kids went through a hard time, but they came out the other side and live good lives now.

We got over the fighting and started to live again. As each year has passed, the divorce has faded and the future has become my reality. It is possible to move on."

Aidan, 37

"I met a girl last week. She liked me and I thought I had a chance with her. Then I remembered that I would have to tell her about my three kids, the mortgages, maintenance payments and the weekend access times... no nice weekends away!

If I met this girl last year I would have given up, annoyed at my wife sitting in our house with my kids. Now, I will give it a go. She seems lovely and, you'd never know, maybe she has kids too..."

Anna, 53

"My divorce papers arrived today. Twelve pages that ends fifteen years of marriage. I thought I would cry but I didn't. I felt a sort of relief when I saw the envelope, which surprised me. I think I am ready to move on. My ex-husband and I have both found this hard. When we got married we didn't expect this to happen, but, now it has, I am ready to get on with it.

I am looking ahead with interest at what the future holds. I couldn't have said that six months ago. I hope I meet someone but, even if I don't, I know I can be happy. I am well and so are the children, and that is what counts."

MOVING ON – THE CHILDREN

Kate, 25

"My dad left my mum when I was twelve. He got remarried really quickly and my mum never forgave him. When he phoned the house, my mum would get me to speak to him. She would stand behind me and tell me to say that he was a cheater and that he didn't love me. She cried a lot and blamed my dad for everything.

My dad used to take me out but then he stopped. He would come to the house and my mum would shout at him. She would scream that he never gave us enough money, she was going to take him to court and that he was a lying cheating ******! She hated him for what he had done to us.

I didn't see my dad again until I was nineteen. I know he had done the wrong thing but I missed him. It might sound funny but I cannot forgive my mum for what she did. She told me things that were not true and tried to stop me loving him. I nearly did, but as I grew up I began to understand more about life. What went on between them should never have been taken out on me."

John, 14

"My parents were so worried about telling us that they were splitting up that they didn't ever manage to say it out loud properly until months after we knew anyway. It would have been a lot better if they had told us earlier. My six-year-old sister used to ask me all the time and I didn't know what to say. I was only nine myself. We knew things were wrong and worried all the time about what might happen.

They told us eventually and then things felt easier. We could ask questions and talk about the future. Mum said that we were still going to be a family and, although they were going to live apart, we would still spend lots of time together. I wasn't quite sure how that would work but I could see she was trying to be positive.

That was five years ago now and we are still a family. Even my dad's new girlfriend sort of fits in. If I had one piece of advice to parents it would be to tell your children clearly as soon as you can. They will only worry if you don't. Let your kids ask questions over and over. That is their way of working it out... and remember that we want you both to be happy, regardless of what you have done."

WHAT KIDS SAY

Kate, 15

"I found out that they were separating when I heard my mum shouting at my dad over the phone. It was awful. I was really upset and I didn't know what to say...."

Bobby, 9

"I didn't really know what was going to happen. I knew things were bad but I didn't know what was going to happen next. My dad moved out of the house. I asked my mum and she started crying. My gran was there so I asked her and she told me that my mum and dad were splitting up. My gran told me the truth. I love her for that."

Susan, 10

"My dad told us. He just said it while he was driving along. He said, 'I am not going to live with your mum anymore. It's for the best. We will stop fighting then.' And that was that. My little brothers started crying and I just said, 'Oh'. He dropped us at the door and went."

Billie, 14

"I would have liked to have known more about what was going on. It would have helped if they had sat down and talked to us. We wouldn't have worried then."

Carla, 11

"I wouldn't want to make the decisions. It would be the same as taking sides and I couldn't do that. I just want to know what is going to happen and that they are going to decide for me."

Colin, 13

"It's better now he has left. They don't fight anymore and the house is calmer. I still worry about if he is alright, but it is better."

Ellen, 14

"I worried that my mum would get a new boyfriend and my dad would find someone else, but they have said that they won't. Maybe they will, I don't know. I just want them to be Mum and Dad."

Johnny, 13

"Some people don't like being separated... I didn't like it when my mum and dad told me they were doing this, but I had to get used to it. People can't live together if they don't like each other. That makes sense to me. So, I am okay with it."

Emma, 5

"They shout at each other all the time. We are moving to another house when they separate. That's just what happens, I suppose. At least the shouting will stop."

Sophie, 9

"I see my dad on Saturdays. I worry that he will get sad if I am too busy to see him, so I am always ready. He is always pleased to see me and that makes me happy."

Dan, 12

"My mum was very sad when my dad left. She cried a lot but then she started getting better. I think she is great the way she coped with it all. I think I love her more now."

Zoe, 15

"Mum and Dad have tried really hard to be friends so we can all be happy. I think it is hard for them but they sort of manage to do it. I think it is cool. They are cool. Both of them."

Amy, 10

"Since my dad left I have got closer to him. He tells me he misses me and we talk about everything. He asks me lots of questions about my life and he has time to listen. He didn't used to, so I like it now."

Matthew, 16

"I really argue with my mum and things aren't the best, but then she has a lot to deal with. Mum and Dad split three years ago. I see my dad all the time. He takes me to matches and we get along okay. Mum has to do the school stuff so she gets it from me. I'm sorry I do that, but I can't help it. I love her really."

David, 13

"I would have been happier to see them both all the time but that is not possible. I spend half my time with each of them. It is a bit of a hassle, but I like seeing them."

ADDITIONAL INFORMATION

This section provides details of a number of websites, which can provide you with specific information on many issues relating to being separated or getting divorced. For an up-to-date list of sites, visit www.livingwithseparation.com.

ADDITIONAL INFORMATION – IRELAND

Useful websites and contacts for advice and services in **Ireland**

www.citizensinformation.ie — - Good general advice on all matters of separation and divorce.

www.legalaidboard.ie — - Advice on free legal services.

www.justice.ie — - General advice on the laws, mediation services and courts.

www.courts.ie — - General advice on the laws, mediation services and courts.

www.flac.ie — - Free legal advice centres.

www.treoir.ie — - Advice and support for single parents.

www.lawsociety.ie — - Advice on solicitors.

www.pensionsboard.ie — - General advice on pensions.

www.fsa.ie — - Information and details of free mediation service.

www.resolvingbooks.com — - A website with information to help children deal with separation, loss, anger, sibling rivalry and other problems.

www.barnardos.ie — - Support and services focusing on children.

www.themii.ie — - Mediation services.

www.chatfirst.com.au — - A website for children who are going through parental separation.

www.helpguide.org — - As part of this site there is a section which provides tips for divorced parents.

ADDITIONAL INFORMATION – UK

Useful websites and contacts for advice and services in the
United Kingdom

www.adviceguide.org.uk - Information on all areas.

www.mediation-works.org.uk - Nationwide mediation services.

www.turn2us.org.uk - Information and advice money.

www.shelter.org.uk - Support for those looking for housing.

www.barnardos.co.uk - Services and support for children.

www.familymediators.co.uk - Information on family mediation.

www.helpguide.org - As part of this site there is a section which provides tips for divorced parents.

www.resolvingbooks.com - A website with information to help children deal with separation, loss, anger and other problems.

ADDITIONAL INFORMATION – US

Useful websites and contacts for advice and services in the
United States

www.divorcesupport.com — General advice which also breaks down into state-by-state information. Includes frequently asked questions.

http://divorce.lovetoknow.com — General information.

www.international-divorce.com — Information on getting a divorce through the international courts.

www.parentingafterdivorce.com — Information on parenting.

www.lawhelp.org — Legal information, including how to access free legal aid.

www.helpguide.org — As part of this site there is a section which provides tips for divorced parents.

www.resolvingbooks.com — A website with information to help children deal with separation, loss, anger, sibling rivalry and other problems.

www.usam.com/services/mediation.shtml — Mediation services.

www.mediate.com — Mediation services.

www.mediationworks.com — Mediation services.

www.chatfirst.com.au — A website for children who are going through parental separation.

ADDITIONAL INFORMATION – CANADA

Useful websites and contacts for advice and services in **Canada**

www.international-divorce.com/ca-usa.htm
- Information on getting a divorce through the international courts.

www.parentingafterdivorce.com - Information on parenting.

www.lawhelp.org - Legal information, including how to access free legal aid.

www.helpguide.org - As part of this site there is a section which provides tips for divorced parents.

www.resolvingbooks.com - A website with information to help children deal with separation, loss, anger and other problems.

www.publichealth.gc.ca - Information on parenting in divorce.

www.fmc.ca - Canadian mediation service.

www.mediate.com - Mediation services.

www.mediationworks.com - Mediation services.

www.chatfirst.com.au - A website for children who are going through parental separation.

ADDITIONAL INFORMATION – AUSTRALIA

Useful websites and contacts for advice and services in **Australia**

www.familylawcourts.gov.au   - Information on family law.

www.frsa.org.au   - Information on family relationships.

www.mydivorce.com.au   - Information on all aspects of divorce.

www.resolvingbooks.com   - A website with information to help children deal with separation, loss, anger, sibling rivalry and other problems.

www.relationships.com.au   - Mediation services.

www.familymediators.com.au/sa   - Mediation services.

www.chatfirst.com.au   - A website for children who are going through parental separation.

www.helpguide.org   - As part of this site there is a section which provides tips for divorced parents.

(8)

A FINAL WORD

In setting out the main stages of separation and divorce, this book has hopefully helped to give clarity to many of the issues you face. Of course, what it cannot do is make the decisions for you. This is up to you.

The effects of separation or divorce do not stop on the day you sign your agreement, particularly if you have children. The finances and asset division, debt responsibility and parenting plan will impact your life for many years to come. Yet, the expectation to move on, put the past in the past and start again is there as well. What makes this possible?

As far as the agreement itself is concerned, it is our sense of fairness that makes any agreement workable and creates the possibility of letting go. Each person's idea of fair play is different and it can be intensely difficult if you feel that you are up against someone who does not share your wish for a balanced outcome.

It might seem that fairness is only about what is finally agreed, but in reality it is more about how you have reached agreement. If each of you has had the opportunity to voice your own opinions, been listened to and got to understand even a little of the needs and interests of the other person, then, not only will you actually have a fairer agreement, but you will have a sense of ownership of the outcome.

There are occasions when taking on the fight and seeking a court ruling is the only way to go; however, the trick is to not escalate an already difficult situation by fighting endlessly over one or two issues. Life really is too short for protracted battles of any sort that leave each or both of you bitter and exhausted, jaded by life and cynical about love.

This is not an easy time, of course not, but you chose this relationship in the first instance and you can choose how you finish it. Maybe your ex-partner will not be as accommodating as you want. He or she may annoy you to a ridiculous degree, but it is still your choice in how you respond, even when things get hot and angry.

It can be difficult to finally have an emotional separation from the person you have been so close to for a good number of years. Not everyone realises that anger is in fact an attachment as strong as love itself. Those feelings of annoyance and outrage can keep the relationship alive even when we think we are ready to move on.

In particularly bitter separations the need for retribution can eat away at an individual for a very long time, infecting everything in their new life beyond the separation itself. Most of us can get over the rows, given time, but the constant burning feelings of revenge will have a more destructive outcome than anything agreed in court.

Detaching from someone we used to love will mean sadness and quite often depression for a while. We need to go through this before we can get to accepting our new independent state. Staying angry can prevent us from going through this natural transition.

You cannot do anything about your ex-partner's behaviour but you can do something about your own well-being and state of mind.

Negotiate the agreement and don't fight the person.

Look to the future, having learned from the past.

Love your children as parents and don't stay ex-lovers.

And above all...

Remember that your future contentment lies in your hands and your hands alone, regardless of any particular outcome.